CODING FOR KIDS

CREATE YOUR OWN APP
WITH APP INVENTOR

DESIGNED AND WRITTEN BY MONICA ORIANI CAUDURO

ILLUSTRATIONS BY LAURA STROPPI

GRAPHIC LAYOUT BY VALENTINA FIGUS

WITH **MIT APP INVENTOR 2**:
WE ARE GOING TO CREATE NEW
APPS FOR YOUR SMARTPHONE
AND YOUR TABLET TOGETHER!
ARE YOU READY?

CONTENTS

Why Learn Coding?

Our book series "Coding for kids" is meant to introduce young boys and girls to the basic concepts of coding. Programming is an ability that is more and more fundamental for the new frontiers of education and is indeed included in syllabuses since primary school. It is then a basic ability, as maths or languages, that goes well beyond the basic ability of using a computer. Programming, indeed, means most of all training our mind to solve problems in a computational way: breaking them down in smaller sub-problems that can be solved in a given order until the final goal is reached. Dealing with kids, it is important that this activity is proposed as a game, fun and engaging, using coding languages created specifically for them.

After having introduced our young readers to the basics of coding with Scratch in the first two volumes of this series, we will now face the world of mobile programming with the App Inventor application. With this, it will be possible to learn how to code different kinds of games, from simple to complex, for smartphones and tablets. Our purpose, as always, is not to train young programmers: putting in contact young boys and girls with coding will be first of all an occasion to let them express their creativity in a different way. It will be a way to find original and efficient solutions to problems, showing them how beautiful it is to give birth to our

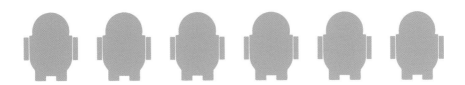

own projects and ideas starting from scratch, from a simple blank page.

With our work, we'd like to encourage kids not to be passively subjected to technology, but to embrace it for what it is: a powerful tool to give birth to our ideas.

The book is composed of four projects for App Inventor 2, that will offer an overview of the opportunities of this programming platform.

Each project leads to realizing a real smartphone app. Every chapter gives, through simple steps, the basic programming tools.

The book also includes an introduction that gives the details of the App Inventor interface, but it is meant to be used starting directly from the first project. At the beginning of each chapter, the kids will find an explanation of the game they're gonna build and the list of materials that will be used (that can be downloaded from the site **www.whitestar.it/coding-app**). After that, a step by step explanation about how to build the game will be shown. Inside each project, some boxes labeled with a magnifying glass will provide further detail of the fundamental concepts that will help to use App Inventor autonomously, while the other boxes contain supplementary information. At the end of each project, the kids will be able to modify the game on their own. Our suggestion is to use the projects described in this book as a basis to build more complex apps, to challenge yourself and thus verify the comprehension of what was explained in the chapter.

THE WEBSITE

As a support to this series of books, we have created a website that you can find at www.whitestar.it/coding-app
Here kids will find characters and backgrounds to customize their projects. Clearly the games work also with different pictures, if they are in the right format.
On our website, every material is in SVG, but App Inventor also supports PNG, JPG and GIF files.

The materials and the games in this book and in the website are property of the Publisher and can be used only for private, non-commercial purposes.

WHAT DOES CODING MEAN?

Coding means giving orders to a computer in a language it can understand.

A program thus transforms the computer in an instrument that is useful for a certain purpose, by simply describing what it needs to do and under what circumstances.

A programmer must be careful in giving precise orders to the computer, and has to think about all possible outcomes, because computers can't think by themselves.

Algorithms

An algorithm is a precise, ordered list of commands to obtain a result. Take as an example how to teach a robot how to reach a certain destination in a grid as the one below. To reach C3 from A1 the robot may for example do the following steps:
Take 1 step to the right for 2 times. Take 1 step up for 2 times.

Here's a very simple algorithm. Of course, you never have only one way to solve a problem!

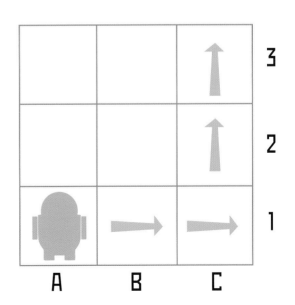

MIT App Inventor 2

"MIT App Inventor is an intuitive, visual programming environment that allows everyone – even children – to build fully functional apps for smartphones and tablets. Those new to MIT App Inventor can have a simple first app up and running in less than 30 minutes. And what's more, our blocks-based tool facilitates the creation of complex, high-impact apps in significantly less time than traditional programming environments. The MIT App Inventor project seeks to democratize software development by empowering all people, especially young people, to move from technology consumption to technology creation."

http://appinventor.mit.edu/explore/about-us

The projects in this book are an introduction to App Inventor 2: each project focuses on some features and interactions with the sensors in your **Android** phone. App Inventor 2 can be used only online, signing in with a Google account. Moreover, downloading the app MIT AI2 Companion from Google Play you can verify how your app develops and try it in real time on your smartphone.

WHAT YOU NEED
- A desktop or laptop computer, with an internet connection
- A smartphone with Android operating system

HOW TO START
1. Download and install from Google Play the app **MIT AI2 Companion**
2. Create a Google account, if you don't have one
3. Log in to the site **http:/ai2.appinventor.mit.edu** using your Google account

CREATING AN APP

PHASE 0 – THE IDEA

Everything starts with an idea. Knowing what you want to do is very important. Not everything has to be sorted out in detail, but it's important that the final objective is very clear. A clear objective lets us define the steps to reach it.

PHASE 1 – DESIGN

When you create an app for your smartphone, you have to create an interface that allows you to use it. You'll need buttons, ImageSprites, images, text fields to start the app, make things happen, update scores and everything else. All these things are called **components**: components are the objects that are visible on your smartphone display. There are other components that allow you to better organize what is visible on the screen, aligning each element horizontally and/or vertically. These components aren't visible but you can see their effect. Moreover, there are non-visible components. Your app may need to interact with sensors in your phone, for example the position one, or with some specific functions such as starting a phone call o computing the gametime using the phone's internal clock.

PHASE 2 – CODING

When you're done preparing the interface, you'll have to program the behavior of your components dragging the blocks you need inside the script area. The components won't function until you assign them programming blocks. For example, if you have put a button with a "start" label in your interface, you'll have to assign a programming block that will make something happen as it is pressed. Programming is "event-based" because everything is triggered by an event, like clicking a button, or dragging the finger on the screen, or time passing.

PHASE 3 – TEST

Connect the smartphone to App Inventor 2 using the app **MIT AI2 Companion** and verify how your app develops in real time. This way, you can realize if the behavior of your components is what you expect, make changes, retry or congratulate yourself!

PHASE 4 – DOWNLOAD

Download the final app on your smartphone and share it with your friends. The phases are consecutive, but not in a linear way: often after a test phase you go back to the idea. After designing the app, you can verify how it looks on the screen of your phone and maybe after the download you can think of something to add or change and then go back to the idea.

Tools

Projects: here you manage your projects, create a new one, import or export projects from your computer

Connect: manage the connection with your smartphone

MIT APP INVENTOR

Projects ▼   Connect ▼   Build ▼   Help ▼

Build: create the app that you can install on your smartphone, save on your PC or publish on Google Play

Help: tutorials, links to forums, documentations, to begin and advance

Links to your projects list

Online guides by App Inventor

Report a problem to the community

My Projects   Gallery   Guide   Report an Issue   English ▼

Enter the gallery of projects published by other "programmers"

Select your language

Designer and Blocks

There are two workspaces. The first one is called "Designer" and lets you insert components in your app.
In this interface you can manage and define the characteristics of the components you use.
The second one is called "Blocks": here you can find visual programming blocks to define the behavior of the component you added to your app in the previous interface.

Designer Interface

Navigation bar between the two interfaces and the app screens

List of available components for the app design

Design area for the interface: drag your components here

List of components you used: from here you can select, rename and delete them

Customization area for the properties of the selected component

Managing area for the multimedia files used in the app (for example audio files)

Blocks Interface

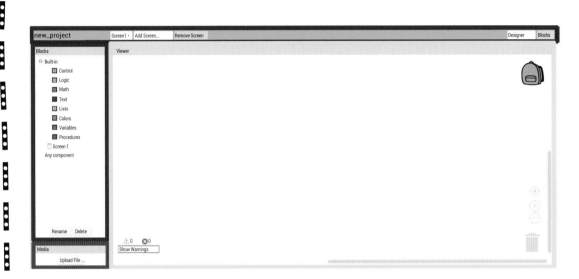

Navigation bar between the two interfaces and the app screens

List of programming blocks, generic and specific for each component used in your app

Workspace: drag here the blocks that define the behavior of the components in your app

Managing area for the multimedia files used in the app (for example audio files)

Dragging some blocks in this backpack, you'll be able to find them also in other projects

Navigation keys for the blocks, to center them in the workspace, to make them larger or smaller

You can erase blocks by dragging them into the recycling bin

It tells you if there are any programming errors, for example unconnected blocks or blocks with something missing

Components

Palette
User Interface
Layout
Media
Drawing and Animation
Maps
Sensors
Social
Storage
Connectivity

The components available for your app are organized in categories: some are visible as buttons or text fields, others are invisible, for example the ones that can order other components in the interface, or sensors.

User interface: it contains elements that allow to build the interface with buttons, text fields, images, selectors...

Layout: here you find the components that allow you to organize the interface components horizontally or vertically.

Media: it contains the components that access the multimedia functions of your smartphone, such as camera, audio playback...

Drawing and Animation: here you find Canvas and ImageSprite components to create videogames and animations.

Maps: components to create maps.

Sensors: here you can find elements that access your smartphone's sensors, such as gyroscope, accelerometer, clock...

Social: components to access social functions, contact list, phone calls...

Storage: components to store data files for the app and access them at a later time.

Connectivity: bluetooth and web. Each component has some properties to which you can assign values, such as the size of the characters in a text field, the Canvas color, the language for media contents and others...

BLOCKS

Blocks

- ⊟ Built-in
  - ▢ Control
  - ▢ Logic
  - ▢ Math
  - ▣ Text
  - ▢ Lists
  - ▢ Colors
  - ▢ Variables
  - ▣ Procedures
  - ▢ Screen1
- Any component

CATEGORIES

Blocks define what the app does. A first selection of the blocks is divided into categories: this selection is common to all components. These are generic blocks that let us manage the conditions that occur when the app is running.

Control: these blocks are very important: they tell your app how and when to do certain things, when to activate something and under which conditions

Logic: these are logic operations that help controlling activation conditions

Math: math operators and mathematical functions to make your app compute

Text: blocks to operate with every textual element (string, in computer terms)

Lists: blocks to manage many values at the same time, grouping them in homogeneous lists

Colors: here you find blocks to handle colors inside the app

Variables: customizable containers for values

Procedures: you can create sets of instructions that have a function in your app, and that you can repeat in various occasions

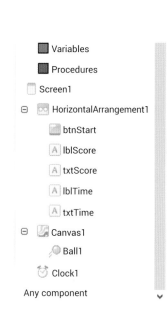

- Variables
- Procedures
- Screen1
- HorizontalArrangement1
  - btnStart
  - lblScore
  - txtScore
  - lblTime
  - txtTime
- Canvas1
  - Ball1
- Clock1

Any component

SPECIFIC COMPONENT BLOCKS

Each component has its own blocks that define its behavior following its intrinsic characteristics and peculiarities. Under the generic categories, you will see that a tree forms with the components used in the app. Clicking on each component it is possible to see specific blocks for each kind of component. A button, for example, will have blocks that manage clicks, a ball ImageSprite will have blocks to handle dragging with the finger on the screen.

TYPES

Different types of blocks are recognizable by their shape and color:

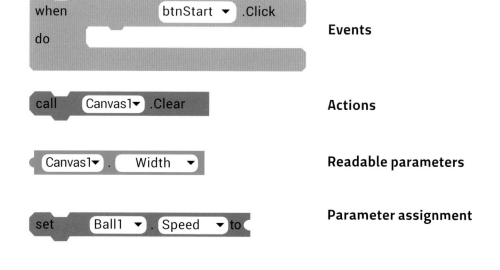

when btnStart ▼ .Click do	**Events**
call Canvas1▼ .Clear	**Actions**
Canvas1▼ . Width ▼	**Readable parameters**
set Ball1 ▼ . Speed ▼ to	**Parameter assignment**

PROJECTS

HERE STARTS YOUR DISCOVERY
OF CODING!

IF YOU HAVEN'T INSTALLED APP INVENTOR YET,
THIS IS THE TIME.
ASK A GROWNUP TO HELP YOU IF YOU NEED!

SOME OF THESE GAMES MIGHT LOOK EASY... TO PLAY!
THE REAL CHALLENGE IS TO PROGRAM THEM,
STARTING FROM SCRATCH.

1.

LEVEL

CRUSH
THE ANT

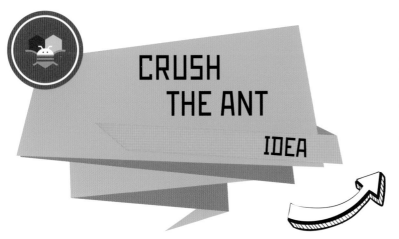

CRUSH THE ANT

IDEA

Ants are invading the phone display! Crush as many as you can to gain points.
The game is timed.

THE GAME

The screen will show a simple green lawn. Clicking on the **Start** button, ants will appear, one at a time, from the right. When you see the ant, crush it with your finger. Challenge your friends!
Who crushed more ants?

WHAT YOU WILL LEARN:

- Move the ImageSprites
- Set a game time
- Start the game with a button
- Assign scores

You'll need some image files: you'll find them in the support site.

DESIGN

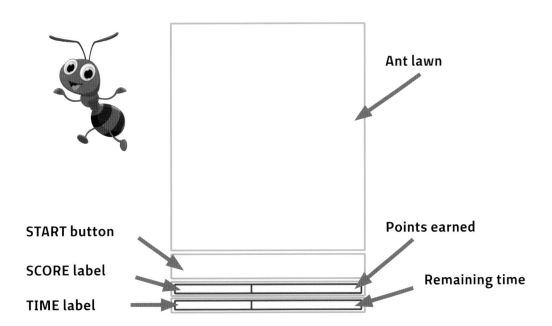

Ant lawn

START button

SCORE label

TIME label

Points earned

Remaining time

This is the layout you'll have to follow to insert the elements of the interface, one at a time.
Connect to App Inventor 2 and click **Projects > Start new project**, choose the name for your app: "**crush_the_ant**" (remember that in the name you can't have blanks, use low hyphens instead) and you're ready to start. The interface you'll see is already the design one.

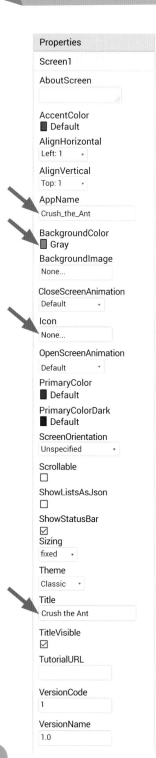

Properties

Screen1

AboutScreen

AccentColor
■ Default

AlignHorizontal
Left: 1 ▾

AlignVertical
Top: 1 ▾

AppName
Crush_the_Ant

BackgroundColor
■ Gray

BackgroundImage
None...

CloseScreenAnimation
Default ▾

Icon
None...

OpenScreenAnimation
Default ▾

PrimaryColor
■ Default

PrimaryColorDark
■ Default

ScreenOrientation
Unspecified ▾

Scrollable
☐

ShowListsAsJson
☐

ShowStatusBar
☑

Sizing
fixed ▾

Theme
Classic ▾

Title
Crush the Ant

TitleVisible
☑

TutorialURL

VersionCode
1

VersionName
1.0

To begin, you have to assign some values to the properties of **Screen1**: Screen1 is the first screen of the App. The properties you have to assign are the name and the icon for the app that will appear on your smartphone, and the screen's title.

Properties	Value
AppName	Crush the Ant
BackgroundColor	Gray
Icon	ico.pgn
Title	Crush the Ant

In App Inventor you can follow two ways to upload the icon, and, more generally, images:

WAY #1 - In **Properties** go on **Icon** and click. A window pops up allowing you to select a file from your PC (you downloaded the project materials, didn't you?). Select the file ico.png and click on **OK**.

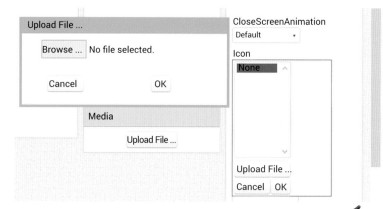

WAY #2 - in the **Media** area (under **Components** on the right of the screen), click on **Upload File ...** A window opens to select the file from your PC. In Screen 1 **Properties** go on **Icon**, click and you'll find a list with the image you just imported. Select it and confirm with **OK**.

THE LAWN

The ants need a lawn to move on: you have to prepare the display with a Canvas.

In **Drawing and Animation** choose **Canvas** and drag it in the **Viewer**.

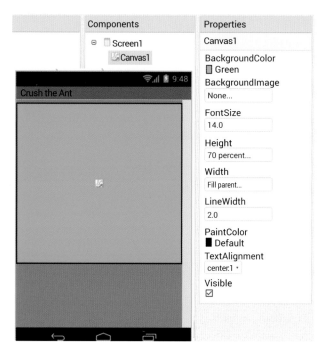

Components	Properties
⊖ ☐ Screen1	Canvas1
☑ Canvas1	BackgroundColor
	☐ Green
	BackgroundImage
	None...
	FontSize
	14.0
	Height
	70 percent...
	Width
	Fill parent...
	LineWidth
	2.0
	PaintColor
	■ Default
	TextAlignment
	center.1 ▾
	Visible
	☑

Crush the Ant

The **Properties** to assign to the Canvas:

Properties	Value
BackgroundColor	Green
Height	70 percent
Width	Fill parent

THE ANT

You'll need just one ant and you can change the image when it is crushed.

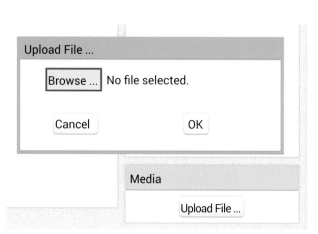

Upload File ...

Browse ... No file selected.

Cancel   OK

Media

Upload File ...

In **Media** click on **Upload File ...** A window opens to select the file from your PC.
Upload the two images of ants that you have found in the project material.

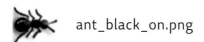 ant_black_on.png
 ant_black_off.png

From **Drawing and Animation** choose **ImageSprite** and drag it inside the Canvas. You can put it where you prefer: the starting point for the ant will be defined in the programming blocks.
In **Properties** you have to assign **ant_black_on.png** to "**picture**". In **Components** click on **Rename** to change the name of the ImageSprite from **ImageSprite1** to **Ant**.

A button will start the game.

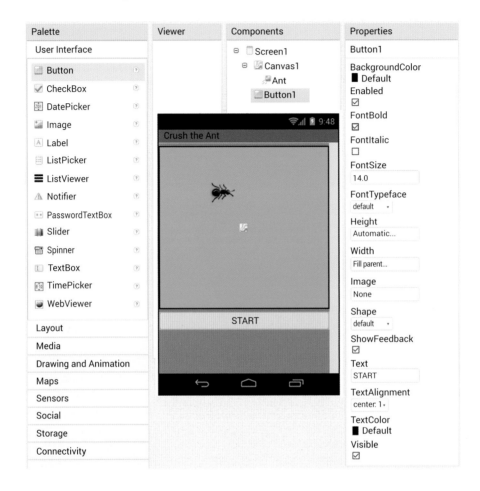

Drag one component **Button** from **User Interface** under the Canvas. In **Properties** assign:

Properties	Value
FontBold	Check the box
Width	Fill parent
Text	START

In **Components** click on **Rename** and give the button the name **btnStart**.

How many ants can you crush in 30 seconds?

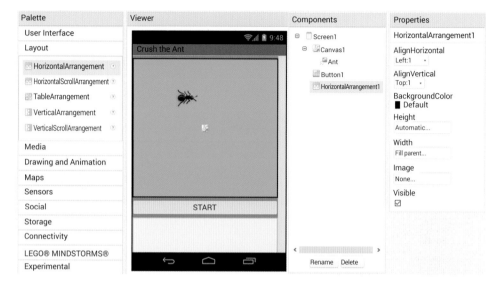

From **Layout** drag **HorizontalArrangement** under the button.
You only have to assign the value **"Fill parent"** to the **property "Width"**.

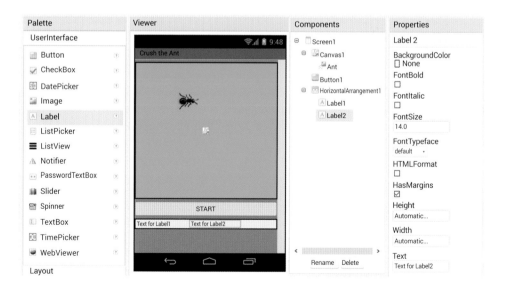

Inside **HorizontalArrangement** place two **Label** components from **User Interface**.

Component	Rename	Properties	Value
Label1	lblScore	BackgroundColor FontBold Width Text	White Check the box 40 percent SCORE
Label2	txtScore	BackgroundColor FontBold Width Text	White Check the box Fill parent 0

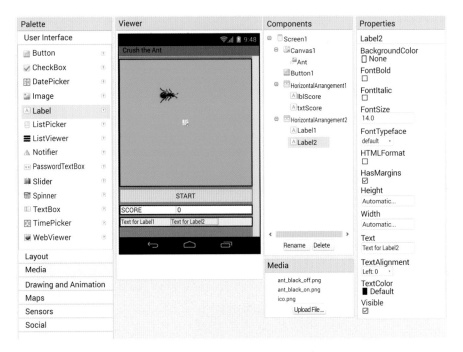

For the time you have to do the same thing. Drag another component **HorizontalArrangment** from **Layout** and place it under the previous one. Inside this **HorizontalArrangement** place two **Label** components from **User Interface**.

Component	Rename	Properties	Value
Label1	lblTime	BackgroundColor FontBold Width Text	White Check the box 40 percent TIME
Label2	txtTime	BackgroundColor FontBold Width Text	White Check the box Fill parent 30

There is a timespan for the game and a pause when the ant is crushed. Since the game works on a smartphone, why not add a vibration when you crush the ant?

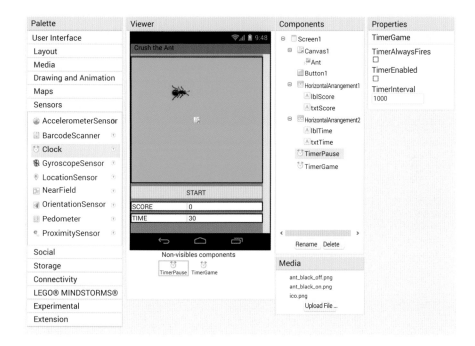

From **Sensors** drag the component **Clock** inside the Screen, no matter where: it will appear under the viewer among the **Non-visible components**.

In **Components** rename **Clock1** to **TimerPause**.
Drag a new **Clock** component and rename it to **TimerGame**. For both, in **Properties** remove the tick from **TimerAlwaysFires** and from **TimerEnabled**.

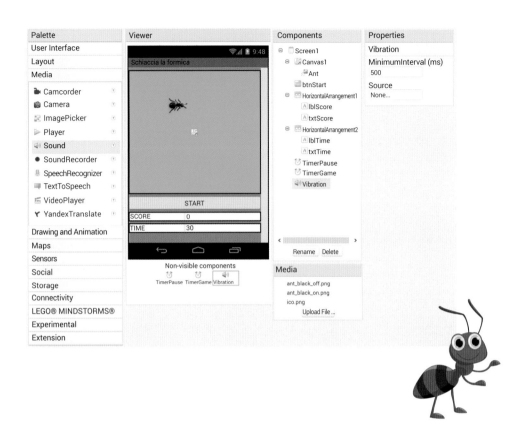

From **Media** drag the component **Sound**: this component too will appear among the **Non-visible components**. Rename it to **Vibration**. There are no properties to be assigned values here.

If you still haven't downloaded the app **MIT AI2 COMPANION** from Google Play, it's time to do it. Now you have to check with your smartphone how the design of your app is going, if all the elements are in the right order and if something is missing from the interface.

Under **Connect** click on **AI Companion**. A window will appear with a QR code, a strange squared code.

Launch the app **MIT AI2 COMPANION** on your smartphone and select the blue button **scan QR code**. Place the phone in face of the computer screen to scan the QR code that is shown: after a few moments the app will appear on your phone display. You'll notice right away that nothing moves, not even pressing the **Start** button: it's time to switch to programming.

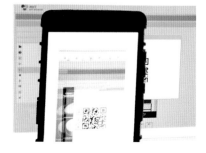

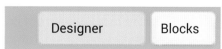

Click on **Blocks** (top right of the screen) and go to the **CODING** phase.

Programming in App Inventor is what is called "event programming": it means that something happens when you carry out a certain action. The first action to program is "what needs to happen when you click on the Start button"?

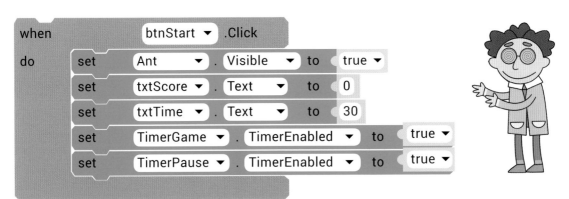

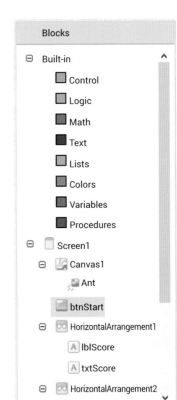

From **Blocks** select **btnStart**, a menu will appear from which you can choose the specific blocks of the component, in this case the **START** button.
Select **when btnStart.Click do**:
it has a "C" shape and will contain what has to happen when we click the start button.

Put inside the following blocks:
1. specific for **Ant**, the block **set Ant.Visible to**, to which you have to connect the block **true** from **Logic**
2. specific to **txtScore**, the block **set txtScore.Text to**, to which you have to connect the block **number** from **Math** and set the value to **0**
3. specific to **txtTime**, the block **set txtTime.Text to**, to which you have to connect the block **number** from **Math** and set the value to **30**
4. specific to **TimerGame** the block **set TimerGame. TimerEnabled to**, with the block **true** from **Logic**
5. specific to **TimerPause** the block **set TimerPause. TimerEnabled to**, with the block **true** from **Logic**

The game time is regulated by the clock that has been renamed to **TimerGame**. As you'll remember, in **Design**, under **Properties**, you'll find **TimerInterval**. This sets the time division, as in clocks: you use it to set the duration of the time span. if you don't change it, the interval lasts 1000 milliseconds, which means one second.

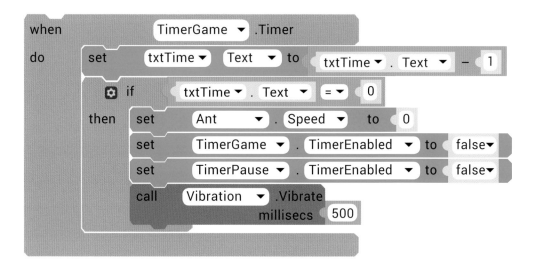

From the blocks specific to **TimerGame** choose **when TimerGame.Timer do**, and inside put the following blocks:
1. from the blocks specific to **txtTime** choose **set txtTime.Text to**, and add the block with the sign "**–**" (minus) from **Math**. In the first space put the block **txtTime.Text**, that you find among the blocks specific to **txtTime**. In the second space put a **number** block from **Math**, with value **1**. This way you remove a second from the game time each time the Timer uses its interval, which last exactly one second.
2. from the **Control** blocks choose the block **if... then**. Near **if** build the condition with the block "**=**" (equal) from **Math**. In the first space put the block **txtTime.Text** from **txtTime**, in second space put the block number from **Math**, with value **0**. Inside **then** place the following blocks:

a. from **Ant**, choose the block **set Ant.Speed to** with the **Math** block number set to **0**
b. from the blocks specific to **TimerGame**, choose **set TimerGame.TimerEnabled to**, with the block **false** from **Logic**
c. from the blocks specific to **TimerPause**, choose **set TimerPause.TimerEnabled to**, with the block **false** from **Logic**
d. from the blocks specific to **Vibration**, choose **call Vibration.Vibrate millisecs** and add from **Math** the block number with the value **500**

How the Ant Moves

The Ant moves on the screen and hits the walls: make it bounce!

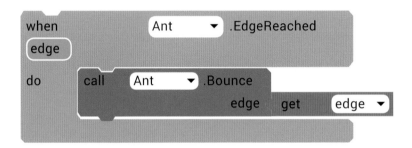

From the blocks specific to **Ant** choose **when Ant.EdgeReached do** and inside put the block, again specific to **Ant**, **call Ant.Bounce edge**, to which you need to attach the block **get edge**. You can find this block by clicking on **edge** on the first block, as in this picture:

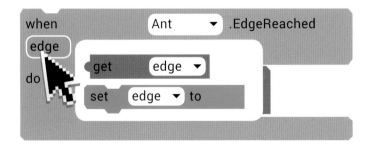

What has to happen when the ant is crushed?

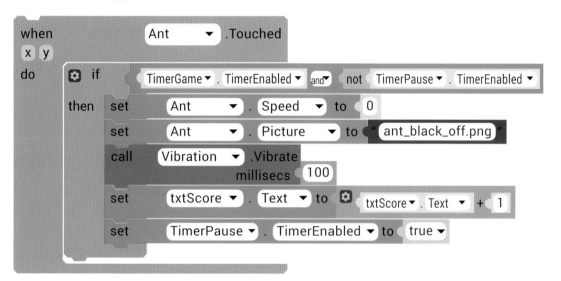

From the **Ant** specific blocks choose the block **when Ant. Touched do** (be careful not to get confused with the similar one you find before in the list). Inside, from **Control**, put the block condition **if... then** to verify if the game time hasn't ended. Build the condition with the **Logic** block "**and**". In the first space put the block **TimerGame.TimerEnabled** specific of **TimerGame**, in the second space put the block from **Logic** "**not**" and from **TimerPause** the block **TimerPause. TimerEnabled**. Inside **then** put the following blocks:

1. from **Ant**, the block **set Ant.Speed to** with the number block from **Math**, set to **0**
2. from **Ant**, the block **set Ant.Picture to** with the " " block from **Text**, setting it to the name of the image of the crushed ant: "**ant_black_off.png**"

3. from **Vibration** specific blocks choose **call Vibration.Vibrate millisecs** and add the block number set to **100** from **Math**
4. from the **txtScore** blocks select **set txtScore.Text to** and add the block with the operator "**+**" (plus) from **Math**. In the first space put **txtScore.Text** from the **txtScore** blocks, while in the second one put the **Math** block number with value **1**
5. from the **TimerPause** blocks choose **set TimerPause.TimerEnabled to** with the **true** block from **Logic**

PAUSE

When you crush the ant, the game stops for a second and then starts again.

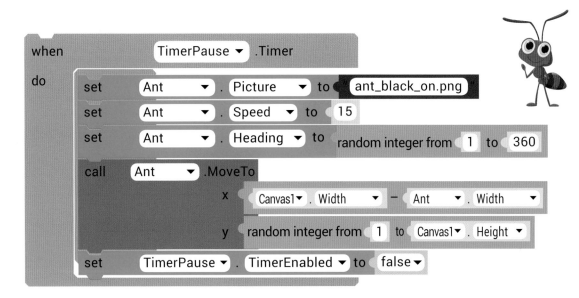

From the specific blocks of **TimerPause** choose
when TimerPause.Timer do and put the following blocks inside:

1. the block **set Ant.Picture to** from **Ant** with the block with the name of the image
   "**ant_black_on.png**" from **Text**
2. the block **set Ant.Speed to** from **Ant** and the block **number** set to **15** from **Math**
3. the block **set Ant.Heading to** from **Ant** with, from **Math**, the block **random integer**
   from 1 to 100 and change the latter to **360**
4. from **Ant**, choose the block **call Ant.MoveTo X... Y...**:
   a) for **x** choose the block "**−**" (minus) from **Math**. In the first space put the block
   Canvas1.Width from **Canvas1** and in the second the block **Ant.Width** from **Ant**
   b) for **y** choose the block **random integer from 1 to 100** from **Math** and replace
   100 with **Canvas1.Height** from **Canvas1**
5. from **TimerPause**, choose the block **set TimerPause.TimerEnabled to**, and get
   the block **false** from **Logic**

The number you put as **Speed** represents the number
of pixels traveled by the **Sprite** for each **movement**.
Interval, which is in the **Sprite properties**, tells **how many**
milliseconds it takes for it to move by the number of pixels
set in **Speed**.

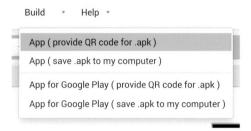

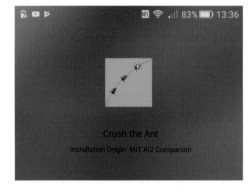

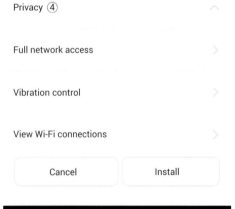

DOWNLOAD

From the menu **Build**, select **App (provide QR code for .apk)**. As before for the connection, a **QR code** will pop up in a new window. Scan it with your smartphone. Be careful! You'll have to allow your phone to install files from unknown sources. Have an adult help and, once you're done, remember to restore the safety conditions.

After a few moments a screen will pop up on your phone, asking you if you want to install the app. Say yes, delete the installation files (it will be asked to you) and the icon of your new app will appear on the screen of your smartphone.

Click on the icon and start playing and challenging your friends!

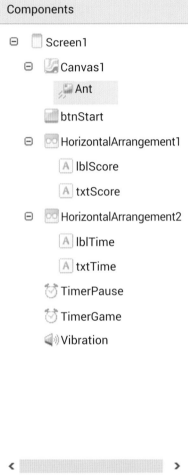

Components

- ⊟ ☐ Screen1
  - ⊟ 🖌 Canvas1
    - 🐜 Ant
  - ▦ btnStart
  - ⊟ 👓 HorizontalArrangement1
    - Ⓐ lblScore
    - Ⓐ txtScore
  - ⊟ 👓 HorizontalArrangement2
    - Ⓐ lblTime
    - Ⓐ txtTime
  - ⏰ TimerPause
  - ⏰ TimerGame
  - 🔊 Vibration

‹   ›

[Rename] [Delete]

Media

ant_black_off.png
ant_black_on.png
ico.png

[Upload File ...]

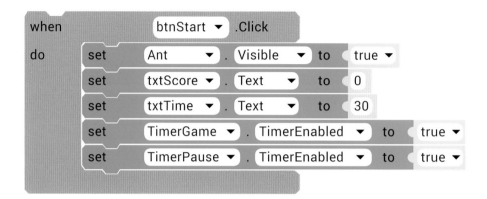

```
when            btnStart ▼ .Click
do    set       Ant      ▼ . Visible  ▼ to   true ▼
      set       txtScore ▼ . Text     ▼ to   0
      set       txtTime  ▼ . Text     ▼ to   30
      set       TimerGame ▼ . TimerEnabled ▼ to   true ▼
      set       TimerPause ▼ . TimerEnabled ▼ to   true ▼
```

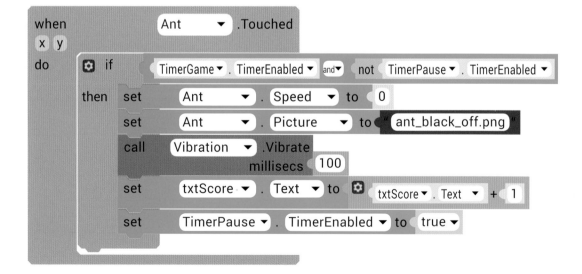

```
when            Ant      ▼ .EdgeReached
edge
do    call      Ant      ▼ .Bounce
                         edge  get   edge ▼
```

```
when            Ant      ▼ .Touched
x y
do    ⚙ if      TimerGame ▼ . TimerEnabled ▼ and▼  not  TimerPause ▼ . TimerEnabled ▼
      then set  Ant      ▼ . Speed   ▼ to  0
           set  Ant      ▼ . Picture ▼ to " ant_black_off.png "
           call Vibration ▼ .Vibrate
                           millisecs 100
           set  txtScore ▼ . Text ▼ to ⚙ txtScore ▼ . Text ▼ + 1
           set  TimerPause ▼ . TimerEnabled ▼ to  true ▼
```

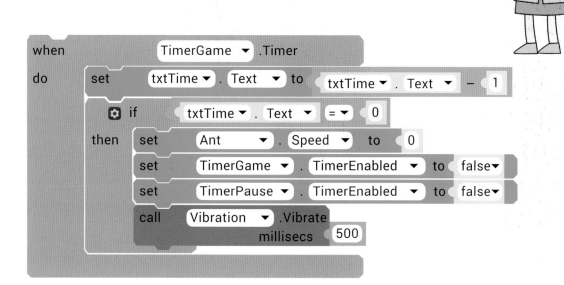

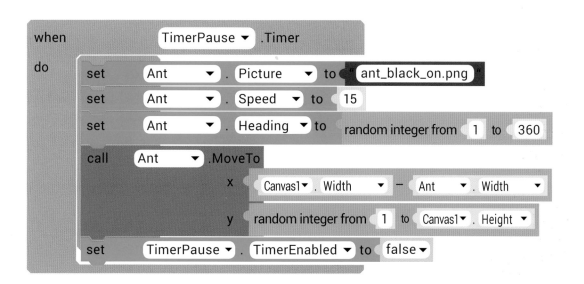

2.

LEVEL

PLANETS TRIP

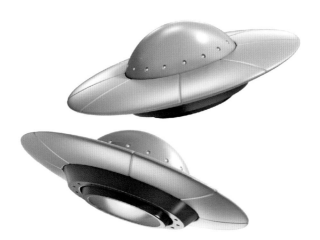

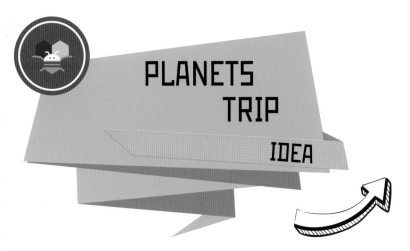

PLANETS TRIP

IDEA

A voyage among the planets. A planet at a time will appear on the display and your starship will have to reach it. The starship moves in the direction and with the speed given by your finger on the screen. The planets are not all the same size.

THE GAME

The screen will have a small white circle, representing the starship, on a starry background. Clicking on the start button the score is set to 0, while time flows from 60 to 0 seconds. The purpose of the game is to reach as many planets as possible in 60 seconds. Each planet will assign a score based on its size.

WHAT YOU WILL LEARN:

- Use variables
- Create procedures that you can reuse in different parts of the game
- Use the time sensor to manage the game time and the planet appearance

You'll need some images, you'll find them all in an archive on the support site.

IMAGES

SOUNDS

In the archive you'll find 2 audio files for special effects too.

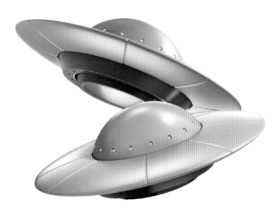

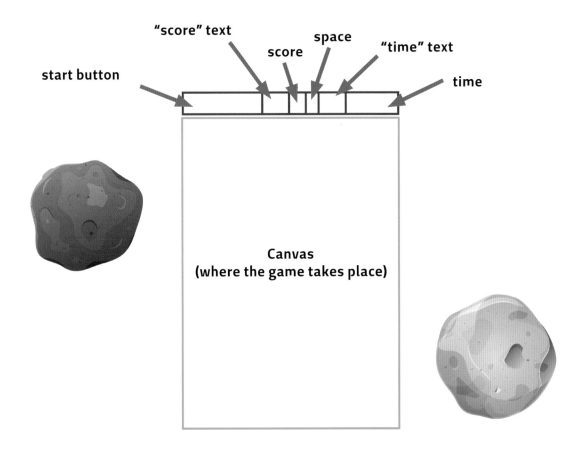

"score" text
score
space
"time" text
start button
time
Canvas
(where the game takes place)

This is the scheme you'll have to follow to insert the elements of the interface, one at a time.

You'll start with the grid that we need to order the elements on the screen: the image for the start game button, the score and the available time.

Under the grid you'll have to place the Canvas, where the game elements will move: spaceship and planets.

Connect to App Inventor 2 and click on **Projects > Start new project**. Choose the name for your app, "**Planets_Trip**" (remember that you can't have blanks in the name, use the lower hyphen!) and you're ready to start.

The interface that appears will be exactly the design one.

Planets Trip

Give a name to your app right away and make it appear on the top left corner. In the **Screen** properties go on **AppName** and write "**Planets Trip**", and the same in **Title**.

AppName

planetstrip

BackgroundColor

☐ Default

BackgroundImage

None...

CloseScreenAnimation

Default ▾

Icon

None
ico.png

Upload File ...

Cancel   OK

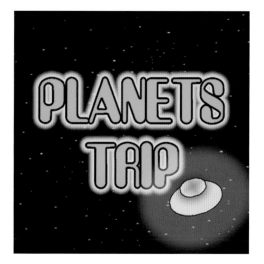

Add the app icon: you can find it in the materials and it's called ico.png.
Do you remember the two different ways you have to add the images that you've seen in the previous project? The **Property** you have to modify is **Icon**. Leave the rest as it is.

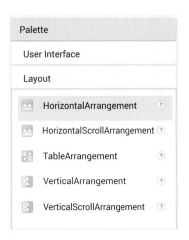

The grid is part of the non-visible elements that are needed to place the elements in the order you desire. Without a layout element, in fact, the elements would end up one under the other.

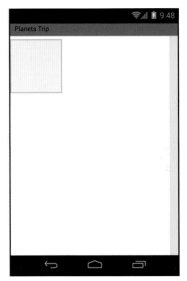

Drag **HorizontalArrangement** in the **Viewer** area. You'll find yourself in this situation. You only have to take care of the value of the **property Width**: you have to set it on **Fill parent** so that it will occupy all the horizontal space.

Check that the selected component is the one for which you want to change properties. You can check it in **Components**: the selected one is the one in green.

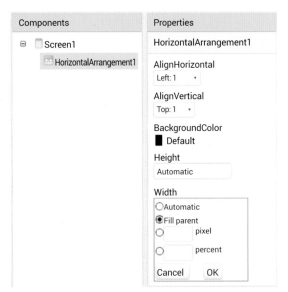

An **image button** is exactly what you need to begin a space exploration.

Drag a new **Button** component and make sure you insert it in the **container element** you added before. Rename it to **btnStart**.

Now modify the **Properties**: first of all delete the content of **Text**. Add the image to the button by using the **Picture property**, and setting it to **imgStartOn.png** which you can find among the attached materials. Now add the file that you will need to **turn off** the button, which is called **imgStartOff.png**, to the **Media** area. You'll use it with the programming blocks.

Score and **Time** should appear on the top of the display, near the start button. As you can see from the layout, you'll need several elements. One for the **SCORE** text, one that will display during the game the score itself, one for the **TIME** text and one that will show the seconds remaining in the game. You'll need an additional one between the score and the **TIME** text to separate them.

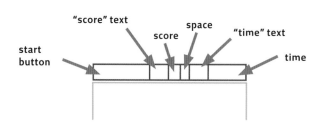

All these elements are of the same kind: the **Label** component.
Place the first one right next to the button that you placed in the previous page.

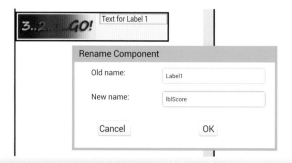

Rename the element to **lblScore**.

In **Properties**:
- check **FontBold**,
- assign the value 18 to **FontSize**,
- write SCORE as **Text**

Add the other **Label** elements, one beside the other. It's likely you won't see the time label, but if you look after the **TIME** text component you'll find it in **Components** and you'll be able to rename it and define its **Properties**. At the end, you can connect with your smartphone through the app **MIT AI2 COMPANION** and see the result of this first part on the screen.

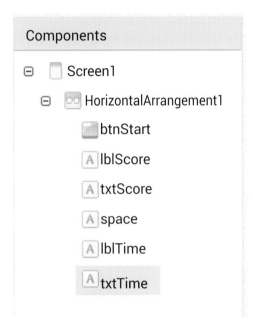

Components

Screen1

HorizontalArrangement1

btnStart

lblScore

txtScore

space

lblTime

txtTime

Component Name	Properties
lblScore	check FontBold
	assign the value 18 to FontSize
	write SCORE as Text
txtScore	check FontBold
	assign the value 18 to FontSize
	write 0 as Text
space	choose Fill parent as Height
	choose Pixel and assign the value 5 as Width
lblTime	check FontBold
	assign the value 18 to FontSize
	write TIME as Text
txtTime	check FontBold
	assign the value 18 to FontSize
	write 60 as Text

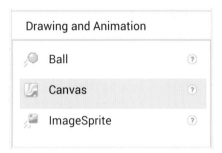

It's time to prepare the game field: in this case we are talking about the sidereal space where your starship will move among the planets.

Drawing and Animation	
Ball	⑦
Canvas	⑦
ImageSprite	⑦

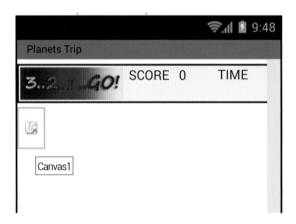

Drag the **Canvas** component below the other elements. It looks really tiny, but giving the right values to the **Properties** it's going to be fine. Rename the Canvas to **COSMOS**.

For the **BackgroundImage** property you have to upload the background **stars.png**, that you find in the materials. You need to make the Canvas fill the screen size, so select the option **Fill parent** for both the **Height** and **Width properties**. In this way you have defined the gamefield.

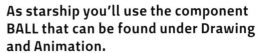

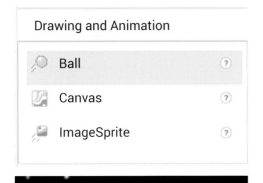

As starship you'll use the component **BALL** that can be found under **Drawing and Animation.**
A ball component is exactly what it sounds like: a circle. You can assign a size and a color to the element, since it is by all means a Sprite.
A Sprite is a character to whom you can give instructions to move inside the Canvas and interact with other characters, that will be other Sprites.

The **Ball** will appear as black on the Canvas, and given the background it won't be easy to see. Change right away the color of this component in its Properties to better see this Sprite on the Canvas. Take the **PaintColor** property and choose **Light Gray**, as metal should be. Another property to which you should assign a value is **Radius**: give it the value **10** and leave the other properties as they are. Finally, rename the component to **Starship**.

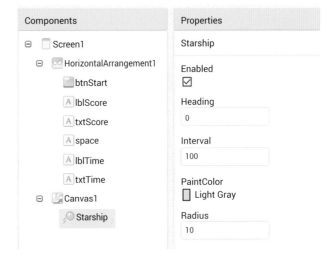

If you have maintained the connection between your smartphone and App Inventor, on your screen you should see the starry space and your grey spaceship ready to be driven to explore the first planet.
Yes, but where are the planets?

THE PLANETS

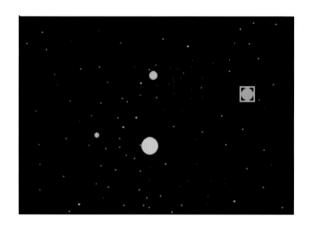

The planets will appear one at a time and won't be all of the same dimension. You'll create three, using always the **ball** component. At the beginning you shouldn't worry about their position: it will be decided through the programming blocks. Here you will just set their size and color.

Component Name	Properties
planet1	for PaintColor choose Orange
	for Radius assign the value 3
	turn off Visible
planet2	for PaintColor choose Cyan
	for Radius assign the value 5
	turn off Visible
planet3	for PaintColor choose Green
	for Radius assign the value 7
	turn off Visible

Oops! The planets have all disappeared from the screen. Don't worry! You'll make them appear again with the programming blocks.

GAME TIME AND PLANET TIME

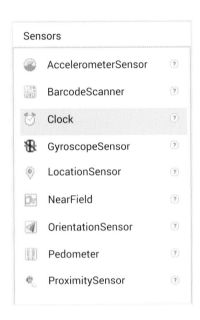

Sensors	
AccelerometerSensor	?
BarcodeScanner	?
Clock	?
GyroscopeSensor	?
LocationSensor	?
NearField	?
OrientationSensor	?
Pedometer	?
ProximitySensor	?

The game time will be scanned by a non-visible element, a sensor that uses your phone's internal clock. You'll need another clock to make planets appear and disappear at each time interval.
In **Sensors**, you can find the **Clock** component: drag it into the **Viewer** no matter where, you'll find it below the **Non-visible components** title. Rename this clock to **TimerGame**.

Non-visible components

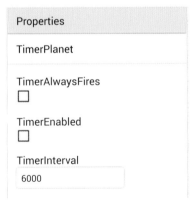

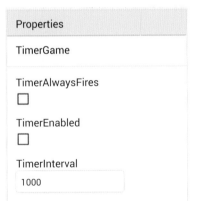

In **Properties**, uncheck **TimerAlwaysFires** and **TimerEnabled**, but leave the **TimerInterval** to 1000: this means that the timer will kick off each second (or every 1000 milliseconds), and this is perfect for the game time. Add another **Clock** the same way, and rename it to **TimerPlanet**. Also in this case, uncheck **TimerAlwaysFires** and **TimerEnabled**, but change also **TimerInterval** to 6000 so that the timer will kick off every 6 seconds.

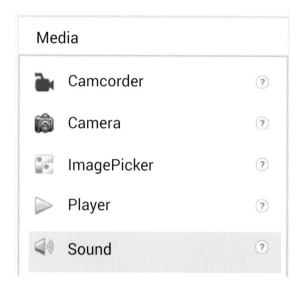

Media

Camcorder		?
Camera		?
ImagePicker		?
Player		?
Sound		?

Non-visible components

TimerGame   TimerPlanet   Planet   Gameover

Sounds help completing the game. You'll have two kind of sounds: one will be played when a planet is reached, the other when the game time is over.
In **Media** you find the **Sound** component. Use two of them and associate them to the **.wav** files that you can find in the project materials. Rename them to **Planet** and **Gameover**.

For the **Planet** component, assign the file **planet.wav** to **Source**. Assign the file **gameover.wav** to the component **Gameover**.

Designer	Blocks

These last additions won't modify the preview on your phone: it's time to switch to the programming phase. Click on **Blocks** and switch to the **CODING** phase!

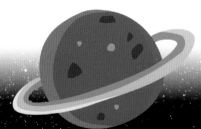

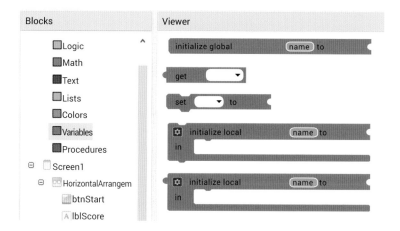

A **variable** is a container of values that can be modified during the game.
The values that can be contained in a variable can be different: words, numbers, but also boolean values, that is to say **true or false**. For this app you'll need a variable that will allow the phone to understand if the game is running or not, that is to say if it is true or false that the game is running.
We need this because some phone functions, as dragging the finger on the screen, should not be activated before clicking on the start button.

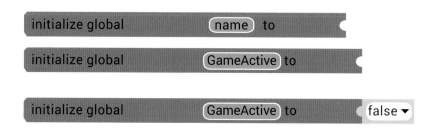

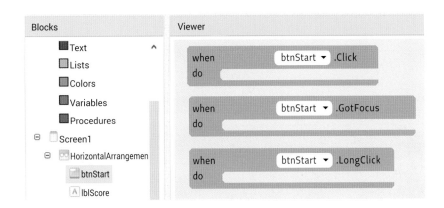

The game begins with the click event on the image button **btnStart**. When the game starts, we need to enable the timers, prepare the text and decide which planet will appear first.

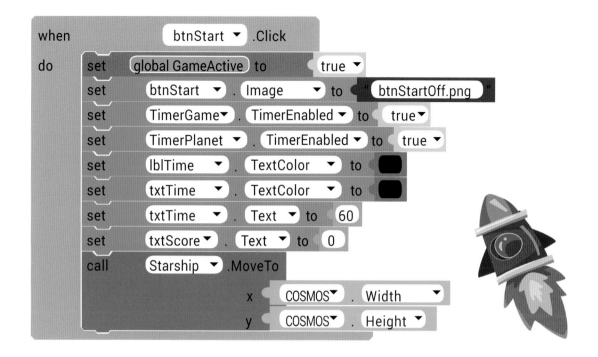

Drag into the **Viewer** the block specific to **btnStart, when btnStart.Click do**.
Drag inside the following blocks:

1. Set **global GameActive** to **true**
2. Set **btnStart.Image to**, specific to the button **btnStart**, and the generic text block with the off image that is called **btnStartOff.png**
3. The GameTimer blocks **set TimerGame.TimerEnabled to** with the **true** block you find in **Logic**
4. Set **TimerPlanet.TimerEnabled to** with the **true** block you find in **Logic**
5. Set **lblTime.TextColor** to **black**: you find the block among those specific for a label; for black, use the **color** block
6. Do the same also for **txtTime**
7. Set **txtTime.Text** to **60**, to set the game time. For the block 60, use the one you find in **Math**
8. Set **txtScore.Text** to **0**
9. The specific block for the component **Starship: Call Starship.MoveTo X... Y...** For X use the **COSMOS** specific block **COSMOS.Width**. For Y use the block **COSMOS.Height**; this way, whatever the size of your device, or of your friend's, the ship will always start in the bottom right corner of the screen

Now test your app! In this moment only the button change seems to work. You have started the timers but the time isn't running and planets don't appear either. You can only see the starship, that is in the bottom right corner, as asked.

STARSHIP
FIRST

The starship has to move when you drag the finger on the screen.
Moreover, it has to follow the finger's direction and speed. However, be careful, it shouldn't move if the time is over.

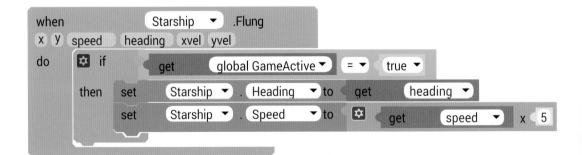

The event that makes the starship move is the dragging of the finger on the screen. In the starship specific blocks you can find the block **when Starship.Flung do**. Put inside it the condition block **if... then** to verify that the game is enabled. In **Logic** you can find the block that allows you to check if a value is equal to another. In the first parameter, place the value of the variable **GameActive** with the block **get global GameActive**; in the second place, the **true** block. Inside **then**, place the starship block **set Starship.Heading to** with the block **get heading**, that you can find by clicking on the word **heading** in the **when Starship. Flung do** block.

Do similarly with speed, getting the **get speed** block by clicking on the word **speed**. This time, put it in a **Math** product block, with **5** as second parameter, so that the ship will be a bit faster.

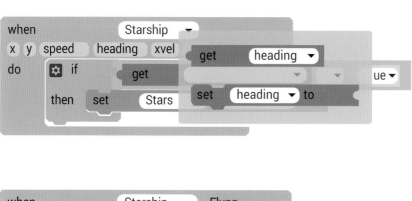

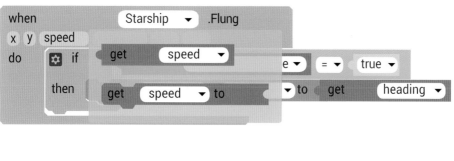

The starship has to stop when you do a simple touch, and bounce when it touches the borders.

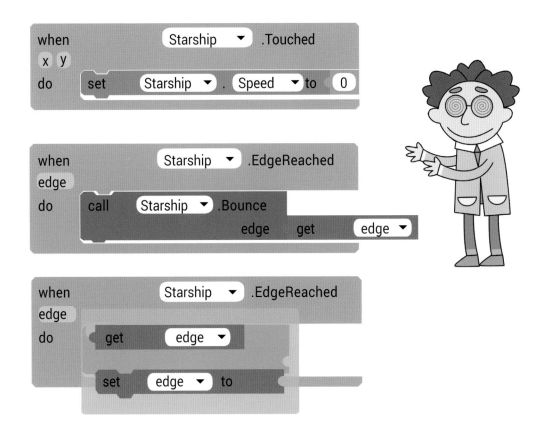

When you touch the starship, it stops and thus its speed is set to 0. Use the block **when Starship.Touched do** and inside the block **set Starship.Speed to 0**.
The event of the starship touching the border has to be managed with the block **when Starship.EdgeReached do**, with the blocks **call Starship.Bounce edge** and **get edge**, that you find by clicking on the word "**edge**", inside.

The planet is still missing, but in any case, you can still put the instruction for what has to happen when the starship touches it.
You have to add score, play a sound, make the phone vibrate and bring back the ship to the bottom right corner.

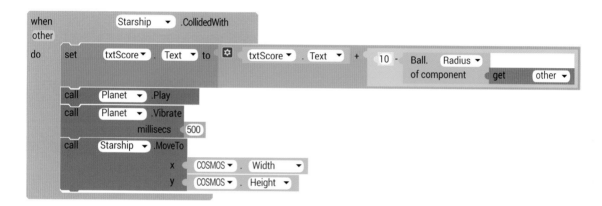

For the event, you'll need the starship block **when Starship.CollidedWith do**.
The first instruction requires the union of different blocks: it's about adding up the score, with the score being dependent on the size of the planet (its **Radius** value). The smaller the planet, the higher the score.
The first block is **set txtScore.Text to**, to be joint with the addition block from **Math**. In the first addend put the block that gives the current score: **txtScore.text**. For the second addend, you have to use a subtraction block: you have to remove from the value 10 the value of the radius of the component the starship is touching.

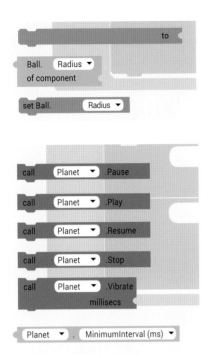

In **Any component** you can find **Any Ball** and its blocks. From this, choose **Ball.Radius of component**. If you click on **other** in the **when Starship.CollidedWith do** block you can find the block **get other**.

Also add the sound blocks (from **Planet**) **call Planet.Play** and **call Planet.Vibrate millisecs** with the value **500**: the smartphone will vibrate for half a second every time the ship reaches a planet.

Bring the starship on the bottom right corner with the same instruction block we used at the beginning: **call Starship.MoveTo X... Y...** with the values **COSMOS.Width** and **COSMOS. Height.**

Game End

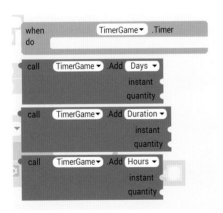

The Game time is regulated through the clock **TimerGame**, which kicks off each second. So, each second the game has to check if the time is greater than 0, and in that case update the time text.

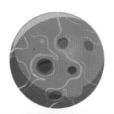

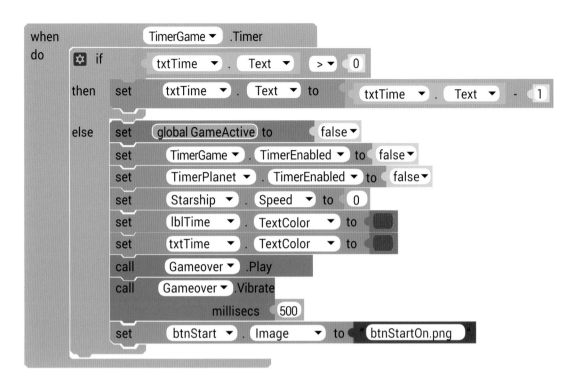

```
when        TimerGame ▼ .Timer
do    ⚙ if        txtTime ▼ . Text ▼   > ▼   0
      then    set    txtTime ▼ . Text ▼  to    txtTime ▼ . Text ▼  -  1

      else    set    global GameActive  to    false ▼
              set    TimerGame ▼ . TimerEnabled ▼  to  false ▼
              set    TimerPlanet ▼ . TimerEnabled ▼  to  false ▼
              set    Starship ▼ . Speed ▼  to  0
              set    lblTime ▼ . TextColor ▼  to  ▉
              set    txtTime ▼ . TextColor ▼  to  ▉
              call   Gameover ▼ .Play
              call   Gameover ▼ .Vibrate
                         millisecs  500
              set    btnStart ▼ . Image ▼  to  " btnStartOn.png "
```

Otherwise, you'll have to set the variable **global GameActive** to **false**, stop the two timers and the starship, assign the red color to the **Time** labels, reproduce the sound assigned to **game over** and make the phone vibrate for half a second. Finally, you'll have to bring back the start button picture to the **on** version, so that you can restart the game.

At this point, the starship moves, the game starts and ends, the score is assigned. But you still have to place the planet! You have to place one planet at a time, randomly. Start from here: you'll use a PROCEDURE, that is to say a group of instructions that you can call all together using only one call.

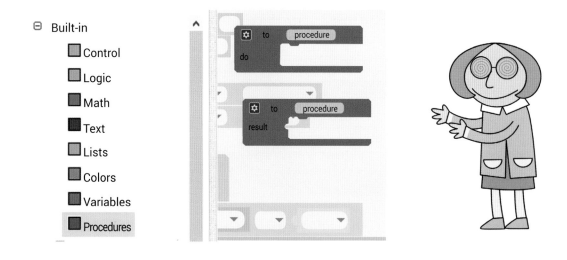

Use the block **to procedure do**: instead of procedure, write **WhichPlanet**, that will be the name of the instruction you can give to call the whole procedure when you need it.

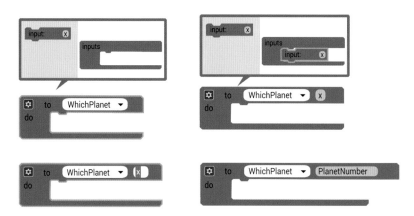

Click on the blue icon and drag the **Input** X from the left part of the panel to the right, inside the **Inputs**. Rename the X with **PlanetNumber**.

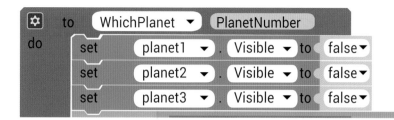

The first instructions set to **not visible** all the three planets. Right after, the instruction **if... then** is needed to evaluate the current value of **PlanetNumber** and thus make the associated planet appear.

 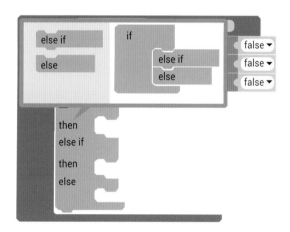

The block needs to be built using an **else if** and an **else**: you have to click on the blue icon and drag the instructions under **if**. The first condition verifies if the value assigned to **PlanetNumber** is equal to **1**. **Else if** verifies if **PlanetNumber** is **2**. In the first **then** you have to set **planet1 visible** to **true**, and the position with random **X** and **Y**.
In **else if** you have to put the same instruction, but with **planet2**.
In **else** you have to refer to **planet3**.

THE FULL PROCEDURE

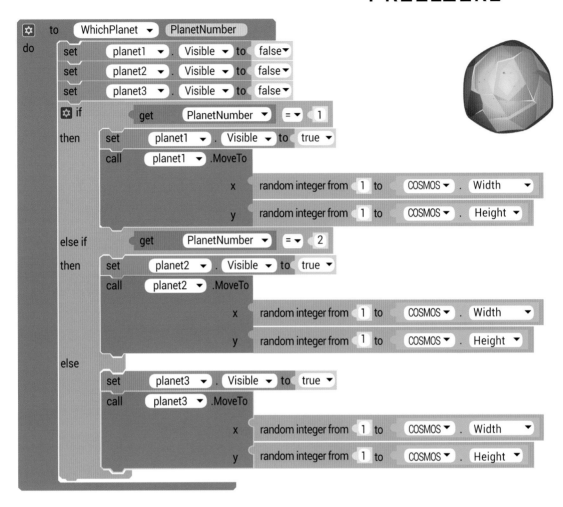

```
to  WhichPlanet ▼  PlanetNumber
do
    set  planet1 ▼ . Visible ▼ to  false▼
    set  planet2 ▼ . Visible ▼ to  false▼
    set  planet3 ▼ . Visible ▼ to  false▼
    if  get  PlanetNumber ▼  = ▼  1
    then  set  planet1 ▼ . Visible ▼ to  true ▼
          call  planet1 ▼ .MoveTo
                x  random integer from  1  to  COSMOS ▼ . Width ▼
                y  random integer from  1  to  COSMOS ▼ . Height ▼
    else if  get  PlanetNumber ▼  = ▼  2
    then  set  planet2 ▼ . Visible ▼ to  true ▼
          call  planet2 ▼ .MoveTo
                x  random integer from  1  to  COSMOS ▼ . Width ▼
                y  random integer from  1  to  COSMOS ▼ . Height ▼
    else  set  planet3 ▼ . Visible ▼ to  true ▼
          call  planet3 ▼ .MoveTo
                x  random integer from  1  to  COSMOS ▼ . Width ▼
                y  random integer from  1  to  COSMOS ▼ . Height ▼
```

```
to  procedure
do
```

```
to  procedure
result
```

```
call  WhichPlanet ▼
      .PlanetNumber
```

Now in **Procedures** you also have the instruction **call WhichPlanet** with **PlanetNumber** as input.

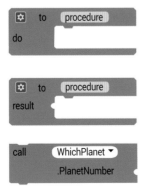

The timer for the planets, TimerPlanet, has an interval of 6 seconds: every 6 seconds a different planet will appear in a different position. The instruction **when TimerPlanet.Timer do** kicks off every 6 seconds.

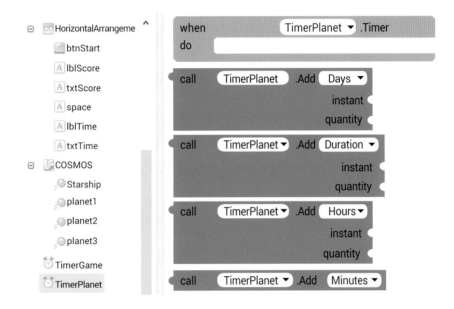

Inside the block **when TimerPlanet.Timer do**, insert the new block that appeared in **Procedures**, your custom procedure **WhichPlanet**, assigning as **PlanetNumber** the block to create a random number between 1 and 3 (the block **random integer from 1 to 3** from **Math**): this way the procedure will evaluate the number that it's given and will make a different planet appear each time.

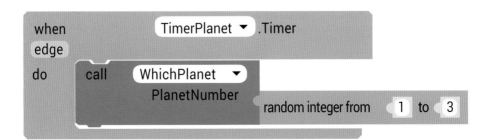

You'll have to call the procedure also in the first block set you built, the one regarding the click on the start button. Otherwise, for the first 6 seconds no planet would appear.

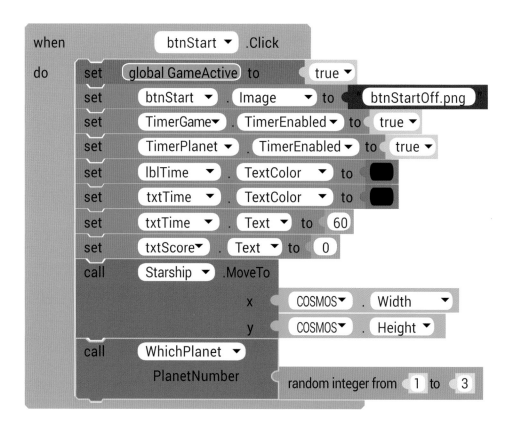

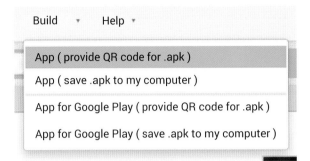

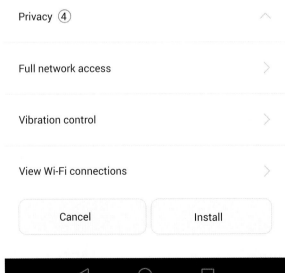

From the **Build** menu choose **App (provide QR code for .apk)**. As for the connection, a QR code window will pop up. Scan it with your smartphone.

Be careful! You'll have to enable the installation of files from unknown sources on your phone: have an adult help you and, when you're done, remember to restore the safety conditions.
After a few moments, a screen will pop up on your phone, asking you if you want to install the app. Say yes, delete the installation files (it will be asked to you) and the icon of your new app will appear on the screen of your smartphone.

Click on the icon and begin your trip among the planets!

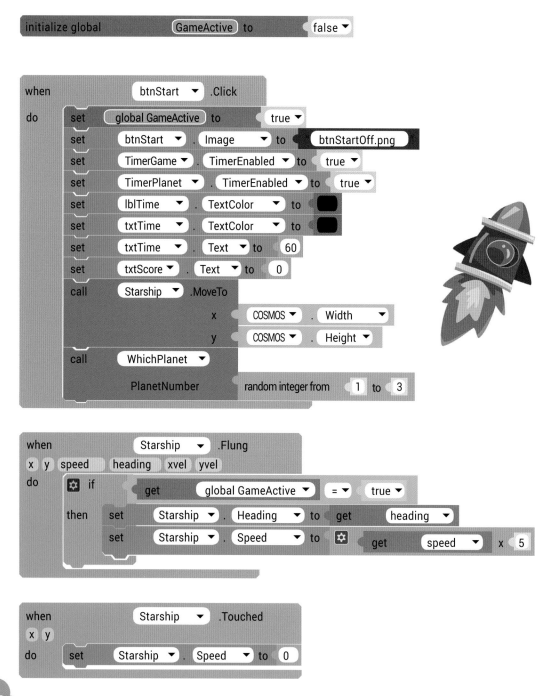

initialize global **GameActive** to false ▼

when **btnStart** ▼ .Click

do
- set **global GameActive** to true ▼
- set **btnStart** ▼ . Image ▼ to **btnStartOff.png**
- set **TimerGame** ▼ . TimerEnabled ▼ to true ▼
- set **TimerPlanet** ▼ . TimerEnabled ▼ to true ▼
- set **lblTime** ▼ . TextColor ▼ to ■
- set **txtTime** ▼ . TextColor ▼ to ■
- set **txtTime** ▼ . Text ▼ to 60
- set **txtScore** ▼ . Text ▼ to 0
- call **Starship** ▼ .MoveTo
  - x **COSMOS** ▼ . Width ▼
  - y **COSMOS** ▼ . Height ▼
- call **WhichPlanet** ▼
  - PlanetNumber random integer from 1 to 3

when **Starship** ▼ .Flung

x y speed heading xvel yvel

do
- if get **global GameActive** ▼ = ▼ true ▼
- then
  - set **Starship** ▼ . Heading ▼ to get **heading** ▼
  - set **Starship** ▼ . Speed ▼ to get **speed** ▼ x 5

when **Starship** ▼ .Touched

x y

do
- set **Starship** ▼ . Speed ▼ to 0

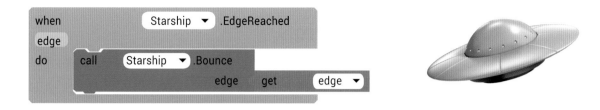

```
when          Starship  ▼  .EdgeReached
edge
do    call       Starship  ▼  .Bounce
                         edge    get    edge  ▼
```

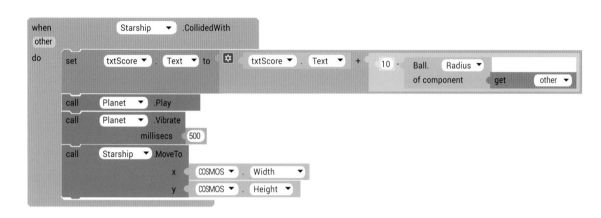

```
when          Starship  ▼  .CollidedWith
other
do    set    txtScore ▼ . Text ▼ to  ⚙  txtScore ▼ . Text ▼  +   10  -  Ball. Radius ▼
                                                                      of component   get   other ▼
      call    Planet  ▼  .Play
      call    Planet  ▼  .Vibrate
                     millisecs   500
      call    Starship  ▼ .MoveTo
                     x    COSMOS ▼ . Width  ▼
                     y    COSMOS ▼ . Height ▼
```

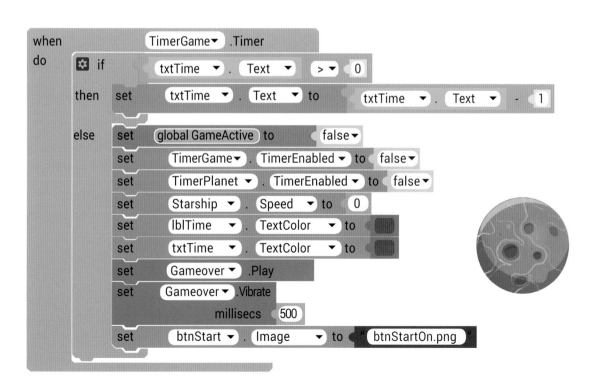

```
when          TimerGame▼  .Timer
do    ⚙ if          txtTime ▼ . Text ▼  > ▼  0
      then  set       txtTime ▼ . Text ▼ to     txtTime ▼ . Text ▼  -  1

      else  set    global GameActive  to      false▼
            set    TimerGame▼ . TimerEnabled ▼ to  false▼
            set    TimerPlanet ▼ . TimerEnabled ▼ to  false▼
            set    Starship ▼ . Speed ▼ to  0
            set    lblTime ▼ . TextColor ▼ to
            set    txtTime ▼ . TextColor ▼ to
            set    Gameover ▼ .Play
            set    Gameover ▼ .Vibrate
                     millisecs   500
            set    btnStart ▼ . Image ▼ to  " btnStartOn.png "
```

73

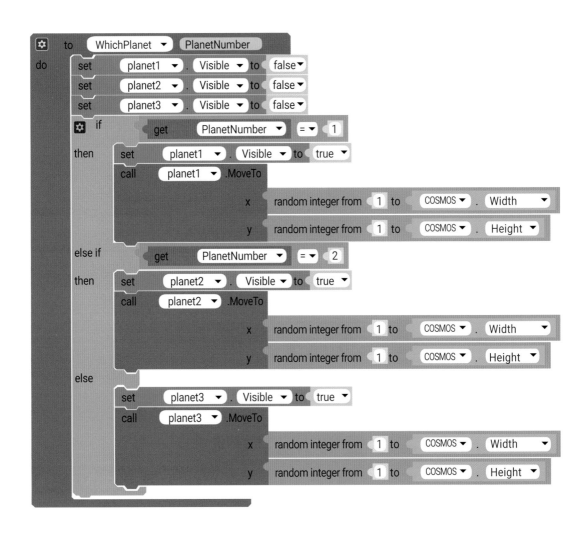

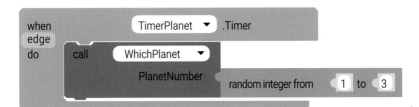

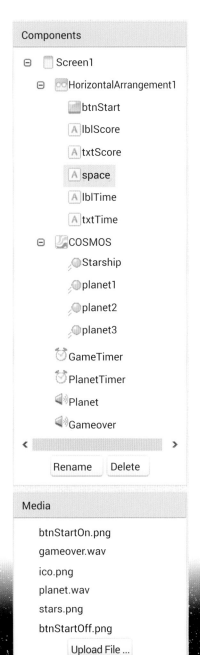

Components

- ⊟ 🗋 Screen1
  - ⊟ 🔗 HorizontalArrangement1
    - 🔲 btnStart
    - Ⓐ lblScore
    - Ⓐ txtScore
    - Ⓐ space
    - Ⓐ lblTime
    - Ⓐ txtTime
  - ⊟ 🖼 COSMOS
    - 🚀 Starship
    - 🚀 planet1
    - 🚀 planet2
    - 🚀 planet3
  - ⏰ GameTimer
  - ⏰ PlanetTimer
  - 🔊 Planet
  - 🔊 Gameover

‹ ━━━━━━━━━ ›

[Rename] [Delete]

Media

- btnStartOn.png
- gameover.wav
- ico.png
- planet.wav
- stars.png
- btnStartOff.png

[Upload File ...]

LEVEL

SMART DRUMS

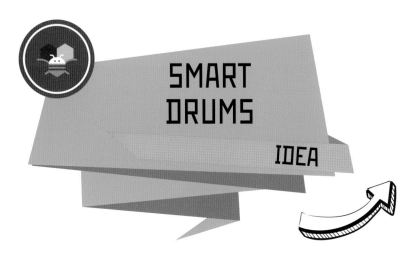

SMART DRUMS

IDEA

I want to play the drums on my phone. The drums are formed by cymbals, drums and a bass drum. Maybe not all of it fits in a screen, so we'll have to choose only a few elements...

THE GAME

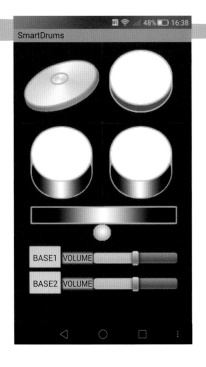

The screen will show five drum elements and two rhythms that will be the base for your musical inventions.

Clicking on each element, you'll hear its sound and the background of the clicked element will change.

You can turn on the rhythms by clicking on the **BASE 1** or **BASE 2** and you need to be able to change the volume.

WHAT YOU WILL LEARN:

- Use images instead of buttons, having them change as they are clicked
- Two different ways to insert sounds
- How to use different buttons: buttons, images and sliders

You'll need some image files and sounds. You'll find them all in an archive on the support site.

IMAGES

SOUNDS

In the materials you'll also find 5 audio files for the different drum elements and 2 audio files for the bases.

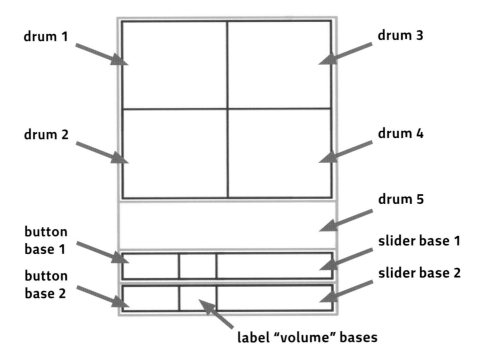

drum 1

drum 2

button base 1

button base 2

drum 3

drum 4

drum 5

slider base 1

slider base 2

label "volume" bases

This is the layout that you'll have to follow to place the elements in the interface, one at a time.

You'll begin with the grid that will order the various elements on the screen: the pictures of drums, buttons, texts and sliders.

Connect to App Inventor 2 and click on **Projects >Start new project**, and choose the name for you app, **Smart_drums** (remember that you can't use blanks in the name, use the lower hyphen instead) and you are ready to begin. The interface you'll see is the design one.

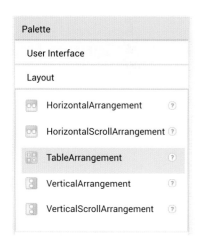

The grid is part of the non-visible elements that are needed to place the elements in the desired order. Without a layout element, the elements would be placed one below the other.

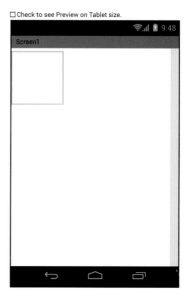

Drag **TableArrangement** in the **Viewer** area. You'll find yourself in this situation. Now define the properties: if you look at the table in the previous page, you'll see that the external table colored in green is composed of 4 rows and one column. These are the values that you need to define in the **Properties** of this component.

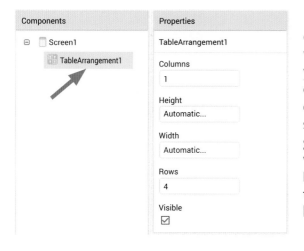

Make sure that the selected component is the one of which you want to modify the properties. Now you have a single element, but later on there's going to be many. You can see it from **Components**: the selected one is the one highlighted in green. In **Properties** place the shown values: 1 for **Columns** and 4 for **Rows**. Leave the other properties as they are, width and height will adapt based on what the table contains.

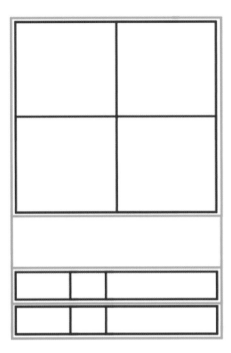

In the first row, the top one, you'll place another table. This is because you'll need to place the elements of the drum in a 2x2 square.

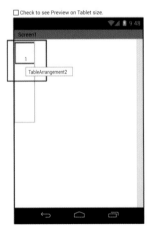

Drag a new **TableArrangement** component and make sure to place it in the first row, as you can see in the image on the left. In the image on the right, you can see what you will obtain.

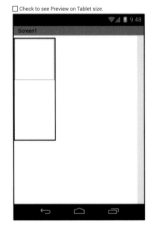

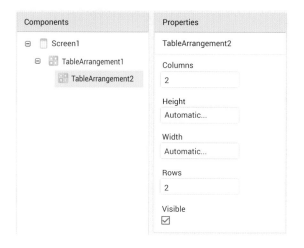

In **Components** the new component is highlighted, but this time you won't need to modify anything in **Properties**: the columns are already 2, and so are the rows.

Let the Drums In!

It's time to place some images and a bit of color! Let's start from the drum elements: cymbals, three drums and the bass drum. Be careful! These aren't simple images, they are buttons "disguised" as images. They have to make a sound when you press them, like a doorbell.

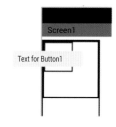

Choose **Button** from the **User Interface** components, and drag it in the first space in the grid. When you drag it, a blue contour will appear on the cell. Then you can release the mouse button to confirm the action.

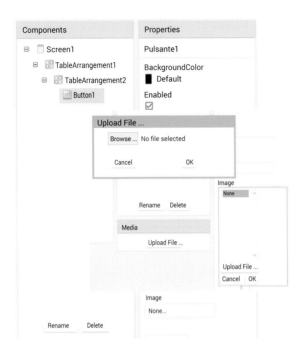

And what about the images? You can associate an image to a button element, you have two ways to do so:

#1 - in **Properties** go on **Image** and click on Upload . A window will pop up, letting you select a file from your PC. (You've downloaded the materials for this project, haven't you?)

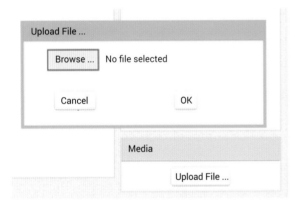

#2 - In **Media** click on Upload File. A window will pop up, letting you select a file from your PC. Then in the button properties go on **Image** and you'll find your image already in the list. Select it and confirm with OK.

The first image is about cymbals and is called **drum1off.png**. To remove that annoying text, find the **Text** field in the button properties, and cancel its content, leaving everything else untouched.

Rename the button, that in this moment is called **Button1**. At the bottom of the **Component** list you'll find two buttons: one to delete the component and the other to rename it. Call the first button **btnDrum1**. It's very important to choose understandable names for each component, because you'll have to assign each of them programming blocks to tell them what to do: if you have given them understandable names, it will be easier to choose the right component to be associated to a certain number of blocks.

Proceed the same way with the other buttons:
1. Drag a **Button** component into the grid
2. Upload the corresponding image and assign it to the button
3. In **Properties**, delete what's written under **Text**
4. **Rename** the button

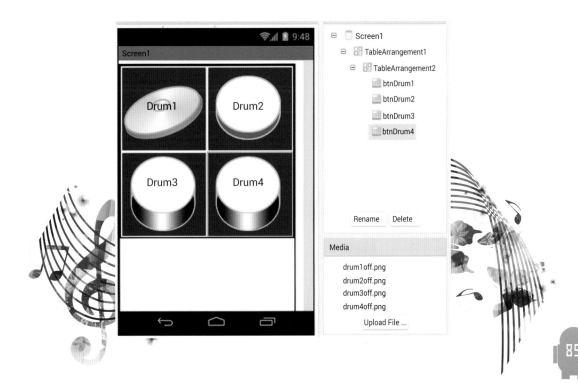

The bass drum is the fifth button and you need to place it in the row below the grid you just assembled, following the previous pages. You'll have to proceed the same way you did for the other buttons, making sure you're dragging the new button in the second row.

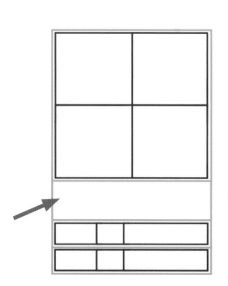

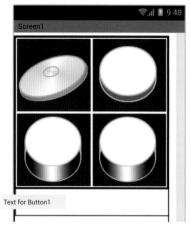

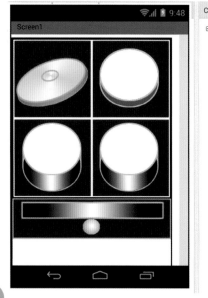

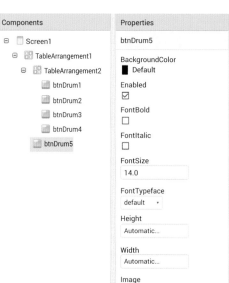

The name of the image is **drum5off.png**. The name to be given to the button is **btnDrum5**.

In the project there are thow bases to choose from to have a background rhythm. For this you'll need three visible elements and two hidden ones.

What is visible:
1. A **Button** element to select the base
2. A **Label** component for the text "**VOLUME**"
3. A **Slider** that will adjust the base volume

What is not visible:
1. A **HorizontalArrangement** component to place all the elements in the same row
2. A **Player** component (you'll find it in **Media**) to reproduce the base

Let's start dragging **HorizontalArrangement** below the bass drum button. In **Properties** choose **Center** for both **AlignHorizontal** and **AlignVertical**. Drag a **Button** in the layout component you just inserted. In **Properties** change **Text** to "**BASE 1**" and check the **FontBold** option. Rename the button to **btnBase1**. Now drag a **Label** next the button you just added and, in its **Properties**, change **Text** to **VOLUME**, turn **FontBold** on and choose **White** as **TextColor** (even if now this makes the text barely visible). Complete the row with the **Slider** component. In **Properties** change the **MaxValue** to **100** and the **MinValue** to **0**; in **ThumbPosition** place the value **50**. Rename the Slider to "**sldBase1**".

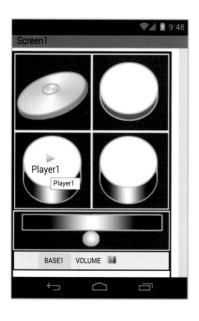

Finally drag the **Player** component anywhere on the smartphone in the **Viewer**. It will appear just below it.

Non-visible components

Player1

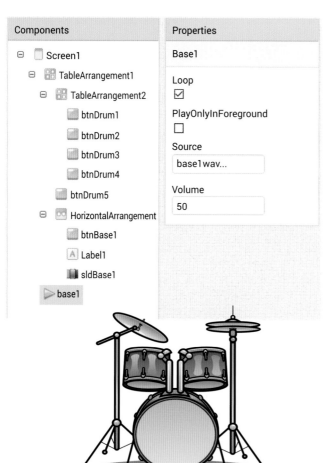

Components	Properties
⊖ ☐ Screen1	**Base1**
⊖ ⊞ TableArrangement1	
⊖ ⊞ TableArrangement2	Loop ☑
▦ btnDrum1	
▦ btnDrum2	PlayOnlyInForeground ☐
▦ btnDrum3	
▦ btnDrum4	Source
▦ btnDrum5	base1wav...
⊖ ▣ HorizontalArrangement	Volume
▦ btnBase1	50
Ⓐ Label1	
▦ sldBase1	
▷ base1	

In **Properties** activate the **Loop** option (so that the base starts again each time) and as **Source** select the audio file **base1.wav** that you found in the attached materials for this project. To upload the file you can follow one of the two methods that we showed you for the images: you can select the file from your PC after clicking on **Source** or insert it in the **Media** area and then select from the list that appears when you click on **Source**. Rename the component "**base 1**".

Follow the same procedure for the second base:

1. Drag **HorizontalArrangement**, remember to choose **Center** for both **AlignHorizontal** and **AlignVertical** properties
2. Place a **Button** with text "**BASE2**" and name it "**btnBase2**"
3. A **Label** with text "**VOLUME**" in white
4. A **Slider** with **MaxValue 100** and **MinValue 0**, **ThumbPosition 50** and name **sldBase2**

DRUM SOUNDS

The drums sounds are other non-visible elements, but you'll hear them well! You need to drag the **Sound** component as you did for **Player**. Rename **Sound1** to "**drum1**" and in Properties select the **Source**: you'll have to upload the file **drum1.wav**. Proceed the same way for all 5 sounds, one for each drum.

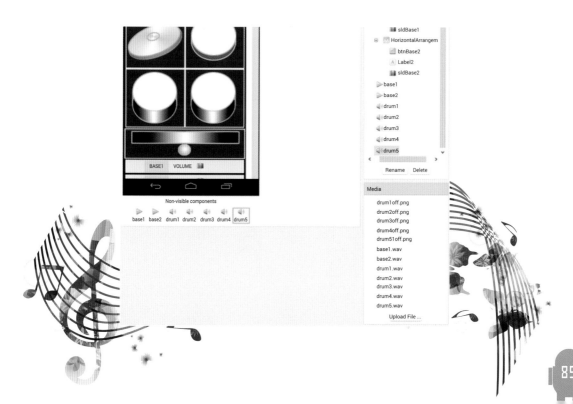

THE FIRST TEST

If you still haven't downloaded the app **MIT AI2 COMPANION** from Google Play, it's time to do it. Now you have to check with your smartphone how the design of your app is going, if all the elements are in the right order and if something is missing from the interface.

Under **Connect** click on **AI Companion**. A window will appear with a QR code, a strange squared code.

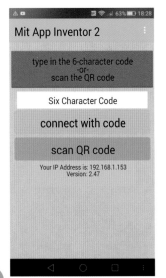

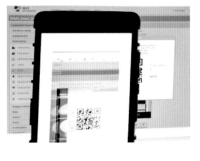

Launch the app **MIT AI2 COMPANION** on your smartphone and select the blue button **scan QR code**. Place the phone in face of the computer screen to scan the QR code that is shown: after a few moments the app will appear on your phone display.

IS EVERYTHING OK?

Not everything is OK: let's check starting from the top.
1. The name of the app is **Screen1**
2. Everything is aligned on the left
3. Where there's no image, the background is light grey.

Go back to your project on App Inventor 2 and keep your cell phone close, so that you can see the changes in real time.

Under **Components** click on **Screen1**: you can't rename it, but you can modify some of its properties that will allow you to correct the problems we have seen before.

1. As **AlignHorizontal** choose **Center**: everything moved, didn't it?
2. In **BackgroundColor** choose **Custom...** and enter the following code: "#002874": this way the color of the background will be the same of the button images.
3. Down in the list you'll find the property **Title**: it's the title that appears on the top left corner. Write "**Smart Drums**".

Look at your smartphone. Now everything is correct, isn't it? But if you press any button, nothing happens: it's time to assign the actions that each element needs to do. Click on **Blocks** and switch to the **CODING** phase.

Designer | Blocks

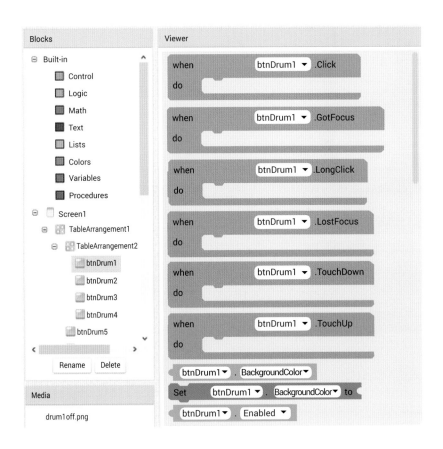

Blocks

Built-in
- Control
- Logic
- Math
- Text
- Lists
- Colors
- Variables
- Procedures

Screen1
- TableArrangement1
  - TableArrangement2
    - btnDrum1
    - btnDrum2
    - btnDrum3
    - btnDrum4
    - btnDrum5

Rename   Delete

Media

drum1off.png

Viewer

when btnDrum1 ▾ .Click
do

when btnDrum1 ▾ .GotFocus
do

when btnDrum1 ▾ .LongClick
do

when btnDrum1 ▾ .LostFocus
do

when btnDrum1 ▾ .TouchDown
do

when btnDrum1 ▾ .TouchUp
do

btnDrum1 ▾ . BackgroundColor ▾

Set btnDrum1 ▾ . BackgroundColor ▾ to

btnDrum1 ▾ . Enabled ▾

Let's begin with the first drum button.
When you click on the button, the image needs
to change and the corresponding sound should
play. At the end, the image should go back
to the original one with the blue background.
In the **Media** area upload the "on" images
of the five buttons: again, you'll find them in the
materials attached to the projects, and they are
named **drum1on.png**, **drum2on.png**, **drum3on.
png**, **drum4on.png**, **drum5on.png**. Select the
component in the list on the left to make the list
of blocks specific to that component appear.

Choose the block **when btnDrum1.TouchDown do** from this list.
Inside it, you should place the action that will change the image, using the block
set btnDrum1.Image to. Then add a generic text block and write the full image
name, **drum1on.png**, in it. Add also the block **call drum1.Play** from the list of
blocks specific to the Sound **drum1**.
For the button click event, choose the **when btnDrum1.Click do** and place again
set btnDrum1.Image to inside, this time with a text block **drum1off.png**.
Repeat this for all five buttons.

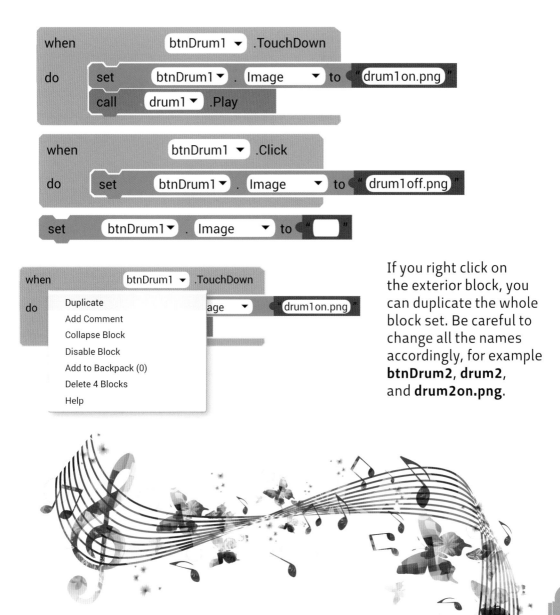

If you right click on
the exterior block, you
can duplicate the whole
block set. Be careful to
change all the names
accordingly, for example
btnDrum2, **drum2**,
and **drum2on.png**.

Second Test

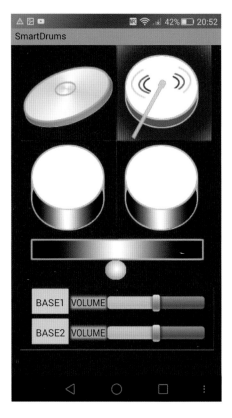

Have you tried your app while programming? Try it now! Play the drums at full volume!

Add the Bases

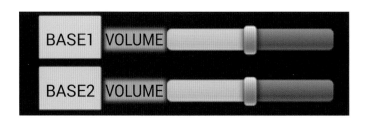

Each base button needs to start its base, or stop it if it's already playing. The slider regulates the volume based on its position.

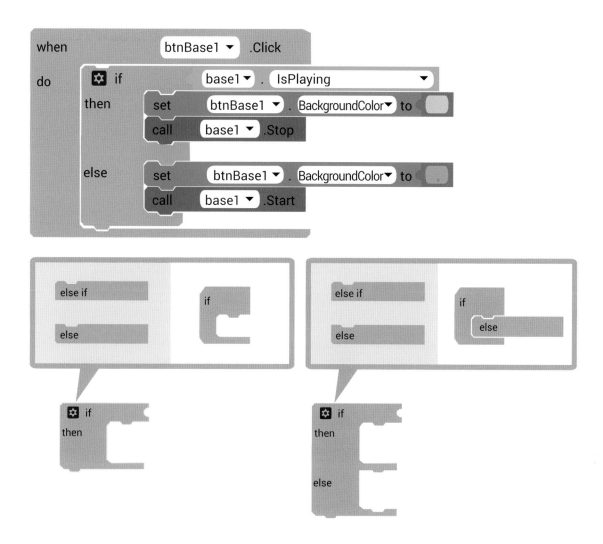

The event that makes the action start is the click on the button "**btnBase1**". Use the block **when btnBase1.Click do**, and put inside the blocks to verify the active music condition.

From **Control** choose **if... then** to which you have to add **else**. Click on the blue icon and drag **else** inside **if... then**, click again on the blue icon and place this block inside the **when** block.

Find the condition that needs to be verified in the specific blocks of **base1**: place the block **base1.IsPlaying** next to **if**. Next to **then** add the block of the **btnBase1** button **set btnBase1.BackgroundColor to** "**Gray**" (you find it in the color blocks). Just below place the block **call base1.Stop**.

In **else** place the block **set btnBase1.BackgroundColor to** "**Orange**" and **call base1.Start**.

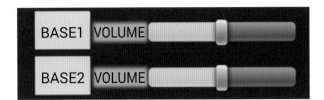

With the finger, move the slider to regulate the base volume.

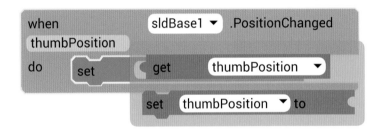

From the **Slider** specific blocks choose **when sldBase1.PositionChanged do**. Inside, place the block from the **base1** player **set base1.Volume to**, then click on **thumbPosition**, get the block **get thumbPosition** and connect it to the previous one.

Repeat these instructions also for **base2**: you can again duplicate the blocks set and select the correct element **sldBase2** and **base2**. Verify that the app is working on your smartphone and prepare for the last operations: downloading the app and installing it on your smartphone.

BEFORE
DOWNLOADING

Only one thing is missing before you can download your app: assign it an icon.

Designer	Blocks

Go back to **Designer** and click on **Screen1**: in **Properties** you find the **Icon** value.

Select the image **icoApp.png** from the attached material: now we're ready to download!

Components

- ⊖ ☐ Screen1
  - ⊖ ▦ TableArrangement1
    - ⊖ ▦ TableArrangemen
      - 🎵 btnDrum1
      - 🎵 btnDrum2
      - 🎵 btnDrum3
      - 🎵 btnDrum4
    - 🎵 btnDrum5
    - ⊖ ⊡ HorizontalArrang
      - 🎵 btnBase1
      - Ⓐ Label1
      - 📖 sldBase1
    - ⊖ ⊡ HorizontalArrange
      - 🎵 btnBase2
      - Ⓐ Label2
      - 📖 sldBase2
  - ▷ base1

Rename	Delete

Properties

base1

AboutScreen

AccentColor
■ Default

AlignHorizontal
Center:3 ▾

AlignVertical
Top:1 ▾

AppName
DEMO_Smart_Drums

BackgroundColor
■ Custom...

BackgroundImage
None...

CloseScreenAnimation
Default ▾

Icon
icoApp.png...

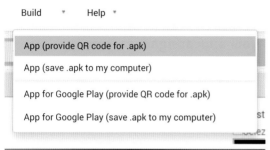

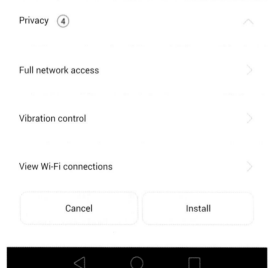

From the **Build** menu choose **App (provide QR code for .apk)**. As for the connection, a **QR code** window will pop up. Scan it with your smartphone.

Be careful! You'll have to enable the installation of files from unknown sources on your phone: have an adult help you and, when you're done, remember to restore the safety conditions.
After a few moments a screen will pop up on your phone, asking you if you want to install the app. Say yes, delete the installation files (it will be asked to you) and the icon of your new app will appear on the screen of your smartphone.

Click on the icon, and start your gig!

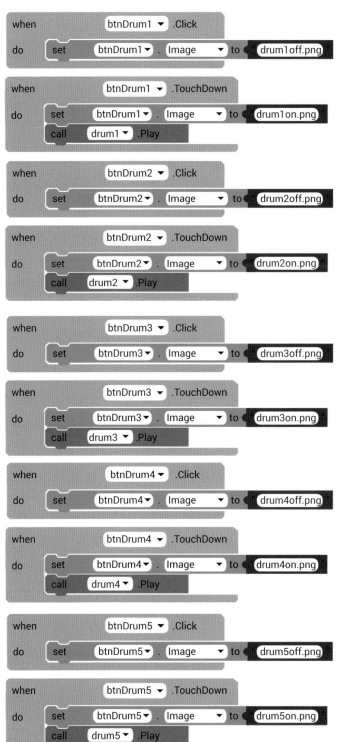

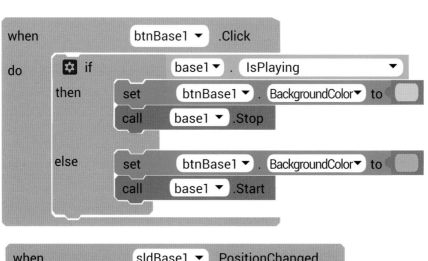

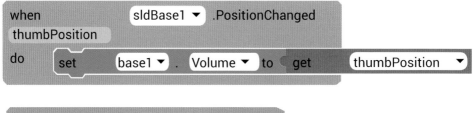

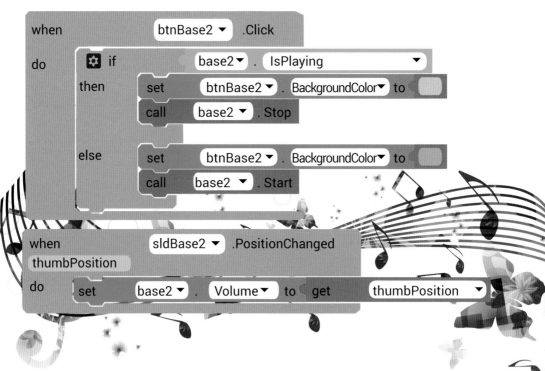

Components

- ⊟ ☐ Screen1
  - ⊟ ▦ TableArrangement1
    - ⊟ ▦ TableArrangement2
      - ▦ btnDrum1
      - ▦ btnDrum2
      - ▦ btnDrum3
      - ▦ btnDrum4
    - ▦ btnDrum5
    - ⊟ ◳ HorizontalDisposition1
      - ▦ btnBase1
      - A Label1
      - ▥ sldBase1
    - ⊟ ◳ HorizontalDisposition2
      - ▦ btnBase2
      - A Label2
      - ▥ sldBase2
  - ▷ base1
  - ▷ base2
  - ◁ drum1
  - ◁ drum2
  - ◁ drum3
  - ◁ drum4
  - ◁ drum5

Media

base1.wav

base2.wav

drum1.wav

drum1off.png

drum1on.png

drum2.wav

drum2off.png

drum2on.png

drum3.wav

drum3off.png

drum3on.png

drum4.wav

drum4off.png

drum4on.png

drum5.wav

drum5off.png

drum5on.png

icoApp.png

4.

LEVEL

EMOJI SOCIAL PHOTO

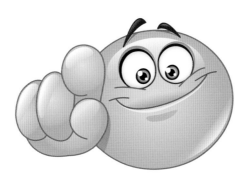

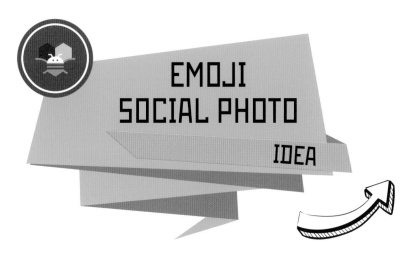

EMOJI SOCIAL PHOTO

IDEA

I'd like an app that allows me to take a picture and stick an emoji on it. Then, maybe, I'd like to write on it where I want and with the color I choose. Then I want to share the picture processed this way on my favorite social networks.

THE GAME

The screen will show what the app can make. In the lower part, five icons will replace the buttons to take a picture, add an emoji, write on the picture, delete to start over again and share the picture.

WARNING: to work properly, this application needs to access the SD Card Archive on your smartphone.

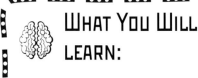

WHAT YOU WILL LEARN:

- Use the choose components
- Use notification windows
- Use various screens and pass selected data from one to another
- Save and send pictures creating a unique name

You'll need some picture files for the button icons and for the screen backgrounds. You'll find them all in the archive on the support site.

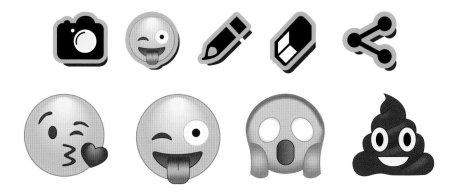

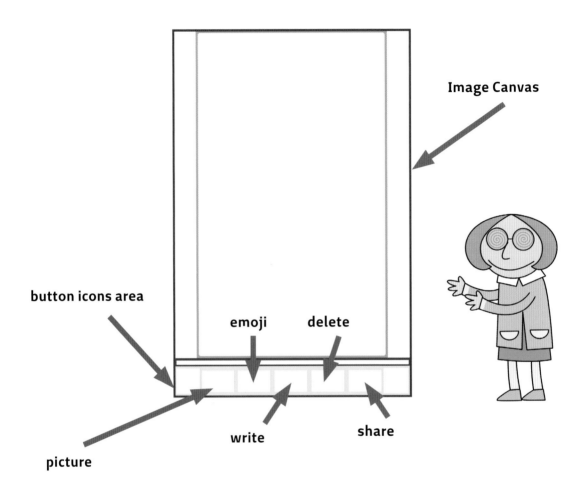

Image Canvas

button icons area

emoji

delete

write

share

picture

This is the scheme you'll have to follow to add the interface elements. Few elements are needed: two canvases and a grid for the horizontal alignment of the elements. Connect to App Inventor 2 and click on **Projects > Start new project**. Write the name of your app, "**EmojiSocialPhoto**" (remember that you can't have blanks in the name) and you're ready to start. You'll be shown the designer interface.

For the first one of the two Screens that will be used for this app you won't need many basic elements:
1. one **Canvas** for the picture that will be shared
2. another **Canvas** will be a colored line to show the color that is selected for the text
3. a **HorizontalArrangement** element to place the buttons in the lower part

Before setting the properties for **BackgroundImage** and **Icon**, download the project materials from the site on your PC. To upload the images on App Inventor and link them to your app, look up the two possible ways shown in the previous projects. Also upload the image **bkgStage.png** that will be used with the programming blocks.

Screen1 Properties

AlignHorizontal	Center
AppName	Emoji Social Photo
BackgroundImage	bkgScreen.png
Icon	ico.png
Title	Emoji Social Photo

Component	Rename	Properties	Value
Canvas1	PictureCnv	FontSize Height Width TextAlignment	40 Fill parent 80 percent Left
Canvas2	ColorCnv	BackgroundColor Height Width	Black 10 pixel Fill parent
Horizontal-Arrangement1		AlignHorizontal BackgroundColor Width	Center Dark Gray Fill parent

Two More Components for Screen 1

A Sprite component, ready to contain the chosen emoji, and a list component to allow us to choose the text color.

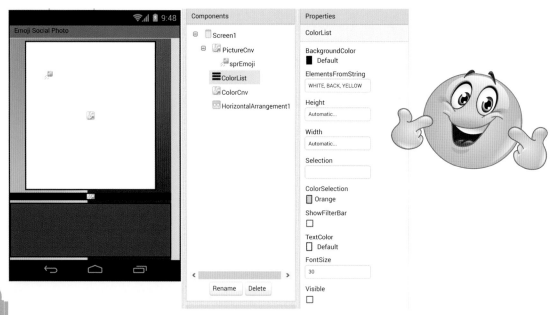

Drag an ImageSprite component inside the first Canvas, **PictureCnv**, and rename it **sprEmoji**: you don't need to do any further change, all you need will be set through the programming blocks.

Drag a **ListView** component from **User Interface** in the space between the two Canvases. Rename it to "**ColorList**" and set its properties following this scheme:

Properties	Value
ElementsFromString	White, black, yellow, orange, red, green, cyan, blue, violet, pink
SelectionColor	Orange
TextSize	30
Visible	Remove the check sign, it will become visible only with the programming blocks.

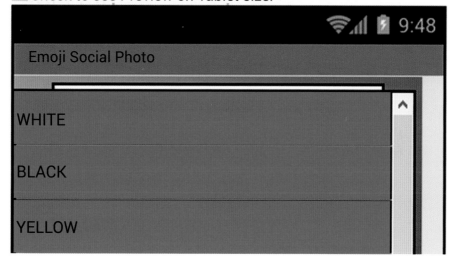

By selecting **Display hidden components in Viewer** you'll be able to see the **ColorList** you just added. Remove the check from it to go on adding components.

Components

- Screen1
  - PictureCnv
    - sprEmoji
  - ColorList
  - ColorCnv
  - HorizontalArrangement1
    - btnPic
    - btnEmoji
    - btnWrite
    - btnDelete
    - btnSocial

Media

- bkgScreen.png
- ico.png
- btnPic.png
- btnEmoji.png
- btnWrite.png
- btnDelete.png
- btnSocial.png

Upload File ...

You'll have to place five button components inside the component **HorizontalArrangement1**. Follow the scheme to rename them and assign them the right image. They won't fit all together, so begin by dragging the first three and then add the remaining two, one at a time. You'll find the images in the materials attached to the project. Remember to erase the text from the **Property Text** of each button.

Button	Rename	Image
Button1	btnPic	btnPic.png
Button2	btnEmoji	btnEmoji.png
Button3	btnWrite	btnWrite.png
Button4	btnDelete	btnDelete.png
Button5	btnSocial	btnSocial.png

NON-VISIBLE COMPONENTS

Non-visible components

Camera1   Notifier1   Clock1   Sharing1

You'll also need non-visible components, that are fundamental to take pictures and share them.

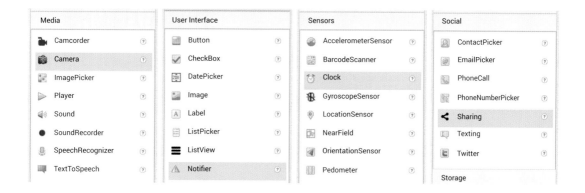

Component	Category
CAMERA	Media
NOTIFIER	User Interface
CLOCK	Sensors
SHARING	Social

You don't need to worry about the Properties for these components: the programming blocks will make you do all the things you need.

A Second Screen

For this project you'll need a second screen: your app will then have a main screen, with all the components you just added, and this other one, that the app will use to make you pick the emoji to be applied to your picture.

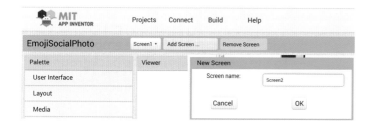

To create a second screen, click on "Add screen…" and name it "scrEmoji".
Confirm by clicking on "OK".

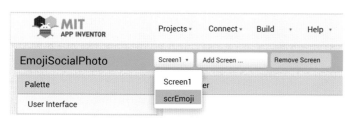

You can select the screen on which you want to work from the drop-down menu in the top left corner.

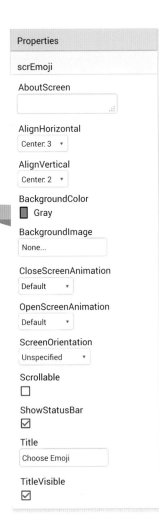

scrEmoji

AboutScreen

AlignHorizontal

Center. 3 ▾

AlignVertical

Center. 2 ▾

BackgroundColor

Gray

BackgroundImage

None...

CloseScreenAnimation

Default ▾

OpenScreenAnimation

Default ▾

ScreenOrientation

Unspecified ▾

Scrollable

☐

ShowStatusBar

☑

Title

Choose Emoji

TitleVisible

☑

For the new Screen, follow this table to choose the right values for the properties:

Property	Value
AlignHorizontal	Center
AlignVertical	Center
BackgroundColor	Gray
Title	Select Emoji

JUST A TABLE AND 5 BUTTONS

In this new Screen you just need an element from **Layout**, **TableArrangement**, and four buttons to be assigned the emoji images.

For the table, you won't need to assign any properties, since it already has two rows and two columns.

Follow the tables you find below to rename the buttons and assign them images (again, remember to remove the text from their "Text" property).

Component	Rename	Picture
Button1	btnEmoji1	EmojiKiss.png
Button2	btnEmoji2	EmojiTongueOut.png
Button3	btnEmoji3	EmojiMunch.png
Button4	btnEmoji4	EmojiPoop.png

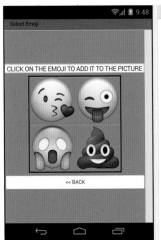

Components

⊟ scrEmoji
  A lblText
⊟ ⊞ TableArrangement1
    btnEmoji1
    btnEmoji2
    btnEmoji3
    btnEmoji4
  btnBack

Above the table place a **Label** element with the text "Click on the emoji to add it to the picture", with **white background**, **FontSize 14** and **FontBold**. (If the text is longer than the lable, lower the FontSize value, for example 12.) Below the table add a button, rename it "btnBack", **Width Fill Parent** and **White BackgroundColor** with the text "<<BACK" in bold.

CODING
TAKE THE PICTURE

First of all, go back to Screen1 from the drop-down menu and click on the **Block** button to access the programming blocks for screen1. The first button makes you take the picture or, better, allows the app to connect with your phone's camera and take a picture. In the programming blocks you have the action **TakePicture** and the event that allows you to control the final result.

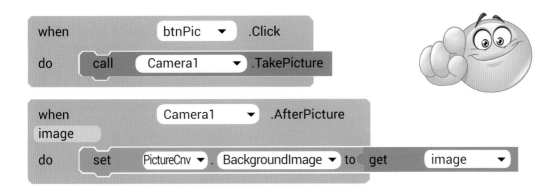

1. From the **btnPic**, drag **when btnPic.Click do**. Place the block inside it, from Camera1, **call Camera1.TakePicture**.
2. From the **Camera1** blocks, take **when Camera1.AfterPicture do**. Place inside the specific block from PictureCnv **Set PictureCnv.BackgroundImage to** and, by clicking on "image", attach the **get image** block.

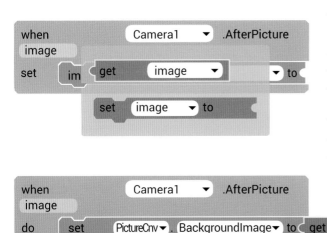

This way, when you click the **Picture** button you activate the smartphone's camera and with the **AfterPicture** event you set the image you just took as a background for your app's Canvas. You can already try and test this function by connecting your phone with App Inventor through the **MIT AI2 Companion** app.

The Emoji button opens a new Screen that needs to "remember" which background image you had and send the chosen emoji to the first Screen. You'll also have to give the instructions that are needed for both Screens. Let's start with Screen1.

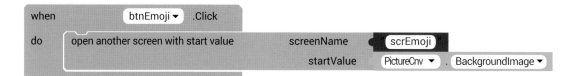

As for the previous button, you'll have to drag the block connected to the event "click of the button", in this case **when btnEmoji.Click do**. Inside, you have to place the block that opens the other Screen (you find it in the **Control** section): **open another screen with start value**. Connect a **Text** block with value "**scrEmoji**" (the screen's name) to **screenName** and, for **StartValue**, the block **PictureCnv. BackgroundImage** specific to PictureCnv.

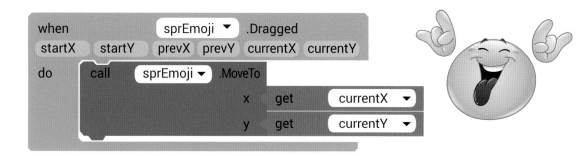

The emoji image will end up in the "sprEmoji" Sprite, and you'll need to be able to drag it with your finger. For this, use the block for "sprEmoji" **when sprEmoji. Dragged do**. Inside it place the block **call sprEmoji.MoveTo**, again from "sprEmoji". For X click on **currentX** and take the **get currentX** block. Do the same to get the **get currentY** block.

Screen1 will receive the value for the emoji to be used from the screen "scrEmoji": you'll have to initialize it.

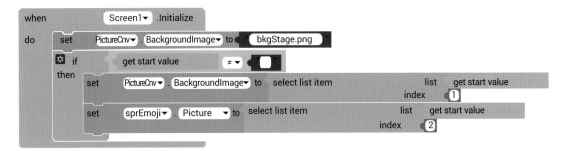

Take the block specific to "Screen1", **when Screen1.Initialize do**. Place the block from PictureCnv **Set PictureCnv.BackgroundImage to** inside it with a text block "**bkgStage.png**".

Then, place a **Control** block **if... then**. You need to compose the **if** condition with a **Logic** block "**=**" and choose the symbol "**≠**" (different): in the first operator choose, from **Control**, the block **get start value**. In the second one, place a **text** block and leave it empty. In **then** place the PictureCnv specific block **set PictureCnv. BackgroundImage to** and from the **Lists** blocks choose **select list item**. Add the block **get start value** for List and a **Math** block with value 1 for **index**. Below this, place the "sprEmoji" block **set sprEmoji. Picture to** with another **select list item**. Again, add the block **get start value** from **Lists** and a **Math** block using this time the value 2 for **index**.

The "scrEmoji" Screen receives the name of the Background so it can re-send it when it closes together with the emoji image, that will be the image of the button that has been clicked.

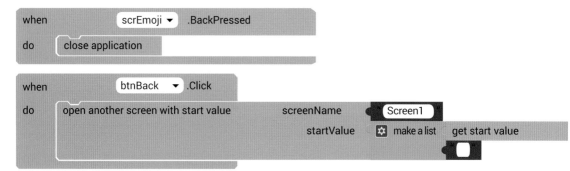

The first block needs to evaluate the case in which you press the **back** button on your smartphone: the application has to close.
The second block is needed to set "btnBack" so that you can go back to the previous screen without leaving the game: let's insert **when btnBack.Click do**. Inside, from **Control**, choose the block **open another screen with start value**. As **screenName** insert a **text** block with "Screen1", as **startValue** let's add the block **make a list** from **Lists**. In the first element, put the block **get start value**, in the second one, an empty text block.

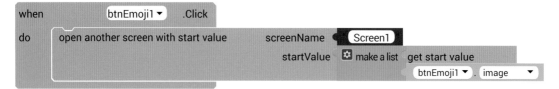

For each button use the specific block **when btnEmoji1.Click do**. Inside, from **Control**, choose the block **open another screen with start value**.
As **screenName** insert a text block with "Screen1", as **startValue** let's add the block **make a list** from **Lists**.
In the first element, put the block **get start value**, in the second one, the specific block from the button that gives back the image value: **btnEmoji1.image**.

> You need to repeat these instructions for the buttons "btnEmoji2",
> "btnEmoji3","btnEmoji4". Pay attention to placing the correct button name
> both in the event block and in the image value one.

It's time for a new test: click on the **Picture** button to take a picture as you did before, then click on the **Emoji** button: choose one of the emojis and move it on the picture.

On the picture, in addition to the emoji, you'll need to place a text in the place and with the color you prefer. You'll need then to have a text box where you can write.

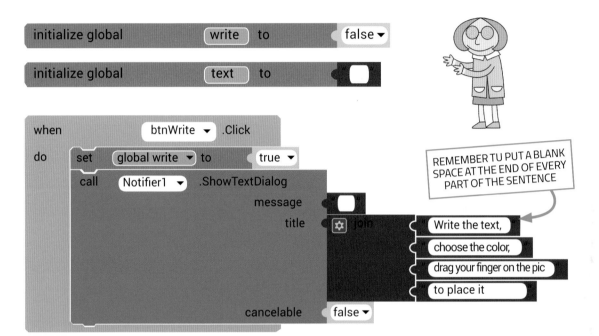

REMEMBER TU PUT A BLANK SPACE AT THE END OF EVERY PART OF THE SENTENCE

Go back to Screen1: you'll have to give the majority of the instructions here. You have to create a variable that allows the app to understand if the button **Write** was clicked or not. From **Variables**, take the block **Initialize global "write" to**, and add a Logic **false** block. Create another variable for the text that you want to write on the picture: you'll call it **text**. Start as usual from the event **click on button** with the usual specific block. In this case the button is **btnWrite** and the block is **when btnWrite.Click do**. Inside, place the variables block **set global write to** with the Logic block **true**. After that, place the block specific to **Notifier1** to open a dialog box **call Notifier1. ShowTextDialog**. For **Message**, place an empty text block. For **Title**, again from **Text**, place the block **join**. The default one only has two blocks, but we will need four of them. No problem: click on the blue icon and drag two more string blocks from the left side to the right one. In each of the four blocks add a text block with the following texts: "**Write the text**", "**choose the color**", "**drag the finger on the pic**", "**to place it**". **(VERY IMPORTANT: remember to place a blank space at the end of each part of the sentence.)** For **cancelable** choose **false**.

If something is written in the notification window, then you have to save the text in the variable and show the list of colors from which to choose, that is to say the ColorList that was placed at the beginning as hidden.

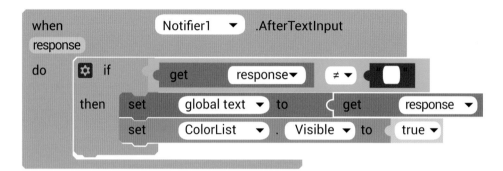

The block of the event is the one specific to Notifier1 **when Notifier1.AfterTextInput do**. Inside the block place, from **Control**, **if... then**. Compose the **if** condition with the Logic block "≠" (different): in the first space place the block **get response** that you can get by clicking on response. In the second space place an empty text block.
Inside **then** place the variable block **set global text to** with again the **get response** block. Following that, use the block specific to ColorList **set ColorList.Visible to** with the Logic block **true**.

The list of possible colors opens, but what happens after the color has been selected?

Inside the specific ColorList block **when ColorList.AfterPicking do** place a block **if... then**: in this way the app will evaluate wich color was selected and will be able to set the text color. You have to add nine **else if**, by clicking on the blue icon. For each **if** place a block "=" from Logic and, in the first space, the block **ColorList.Selection**. In the second space write with a **Text** block all the colors from the list: **white**, **black**, **yellow**, **orange**, **red**, **green**, **cyan**, **blue**, **violet**, **pink**. In **then** place the **PictureCnv** block **set PictureCnv.PaintColor to** with the corresponding color block.

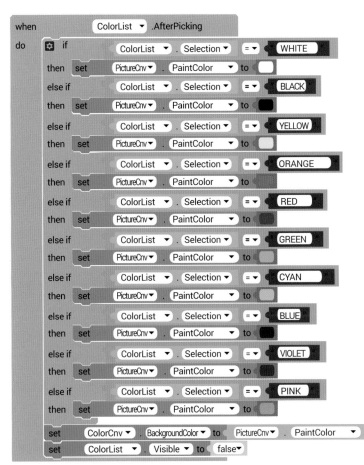

After the last **if...then** place a block specific to **ColorCnv**, **set ColorCnv. BackgroundColor to** with the block **PictureCnv.PaintColor**. This way the line above the buttons will be of the same color chosen for the text. Finally, place **set ColorList. Visible** to **false**.

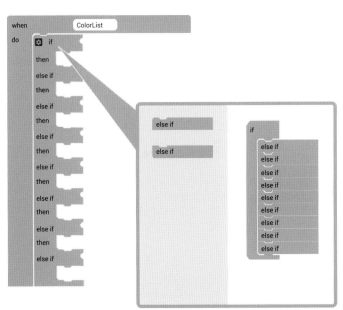

To place the text on the picture you just have to drag it with your finger to the desired position.

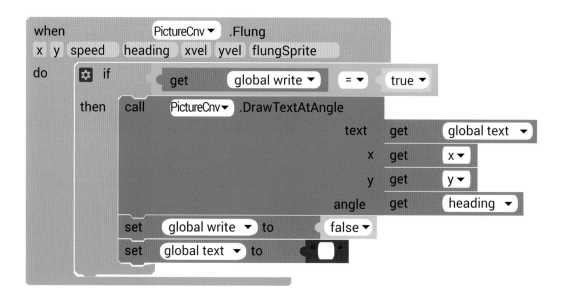

The event of the finger dragged on the screen is intercepted by the block specific to the canvas PictureCnv **when PictureCnv.Flung do**. Inside place an **if... then** block. Compose the **if** condition with a Logic block "**=**": as first operator place the variable block **get global write** and as second operator the Logic block **true**.
Inside **then** place the block specific to PictureCnv **call PictureCnv.DrawTextAtAngle.** In **text**, place the variable block **get global text**: for X take the block **get X** by clicking on the X in the **when PictureCnv.Flung do** block. Do the same for Y and for **angle** get the block **get heading**. After that, place the variable block **set global write to false** and the variable block **set global text to** with an empty text block.

How about trying this new function as well? Connect with your smartphone and try and write what you want!

DELETE

A button to delete all and start from the beginning.

Inside the block specific to the button **btnDelete**, **when btnDelete.Click do**, place the following blocks:
1. **Set PictureCnv.BackgroundImage to** with a text block **"bkgStage.png"**
2. **Set sprEmoji.Picture to " "**
3. **Call PictureCnv.Clear**

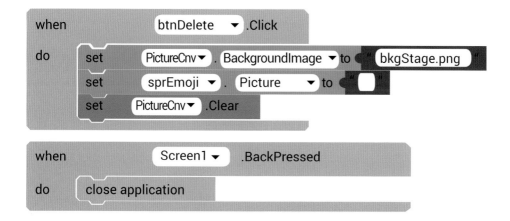

Within the block specific to Screen1 **when Screen1.BackPressed** place the **Control** block **close application**: the application will close when you press the back button on your smartphone.

Why take a picture, stick an emoji on it, write on it, if you can't share it on social media or as a message?

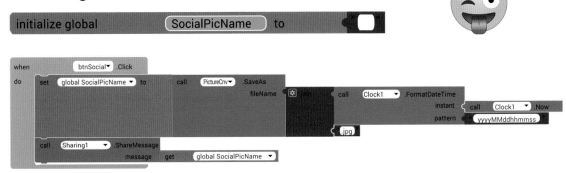

Also in this case we need a variable. It will contain the name of the picture to share. What is saved is the Canvas PictureCnv as it is, with its background picture, the Emoji sprite and the text.

Take the block **initialize global SocialPicName to** and attach an empty text block to it. Then take the block specific to the btnSocial button **when btnSocial.Click do** and inside it place the variable block **set global SocialPicName to** and connect it with the following blocks:

1. from **PictureCanvas, call PictureCnv.SaveAs**
2. **join**, from Text
   a. for the first value of **join** place **call Clock1.FormatDateTime**
      I. as **instant** place **call Clock1.Now**
      II. as **pattern** place a text block with this value: "**yyyyMMddhhmmss**", this way you'll have an image with a unique name formed by the year, the month, the day, the hour, the minutes and the seconds of the moment you save it.
   b. for the second value of **join** place a Text block "**.jpg**"

Finally, place the specific block of Sharing1 **call Sharing1.ShareMessage**. In the message field place the **Variables** block **get global SocialPicName**.

From the **Build** menu choose **App (provide QR code for .apk)**. As for the connection, a QR code window will pop up. Scan it with your smartphone.

Be careful! You'll have to enable the installation of files from unknown sources on your phone: have an adult help you and remember, when you're done, to restore the safety conditions.
After a few moments a screen will pop up on your phone, asking you if you want to install the app.
Say yes, delete the installation files (it will be asked to you) and the icon of your new app will appear on the screen of your smartphone.
Click on the icon, create your own image (be careful: remember to always insert the emoji before the text) and share it with your friends!

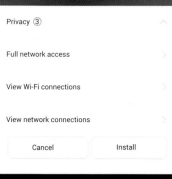

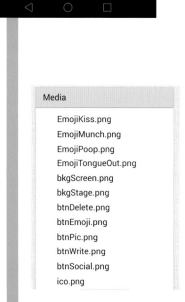

Components and Media files

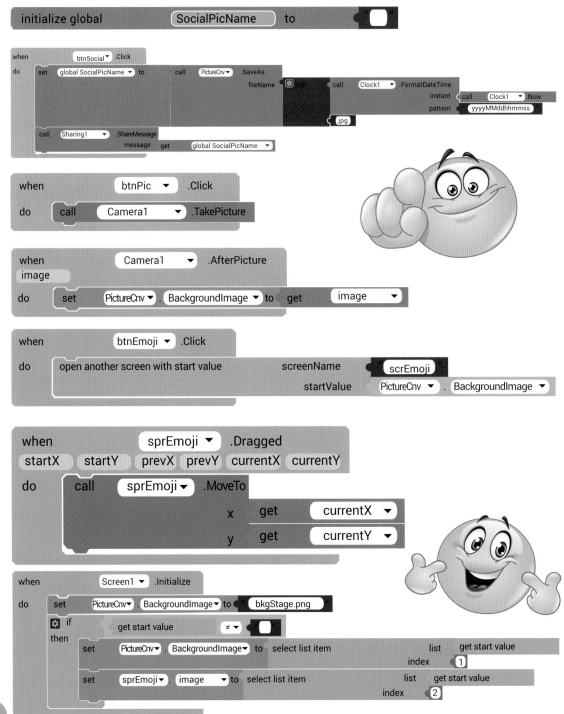

initialize global SocialPicName to

when btnSocial .Click
do set global SocialPicName to call PictureCnv .SaveAs
fileName join call Clock1 .FormatDateTime
instant call Clock1 .Now
pattern yyyyMMddhhmmss
.jpg
call Sharing1 .ShareMessage
message get global SocialPicName

when btnPic .Click
do call Camera1 .TakePicture

when Camera1 .AfterPicture
image
do set PictureCnv . BackgroundImage to get image

when btnEmoji .Click
do open another screen with start value
screenName scrEmoji
startValue PictureCnv . BackgroundImage

when sprEmoji .Dragged
startX startY prevX prevY currentX currentY
do call sprEmoji .MoveTo
x get currentX
y get currentY

when Screen1 .Initialize
do set PictureCnv . BackgroundImage to bkgStage.png
if get start value ≠
then
set PictureCnv . BackgroundImage to select list item list get start value
index 1
set sprEmoji . image to select list item list get start value
index 2

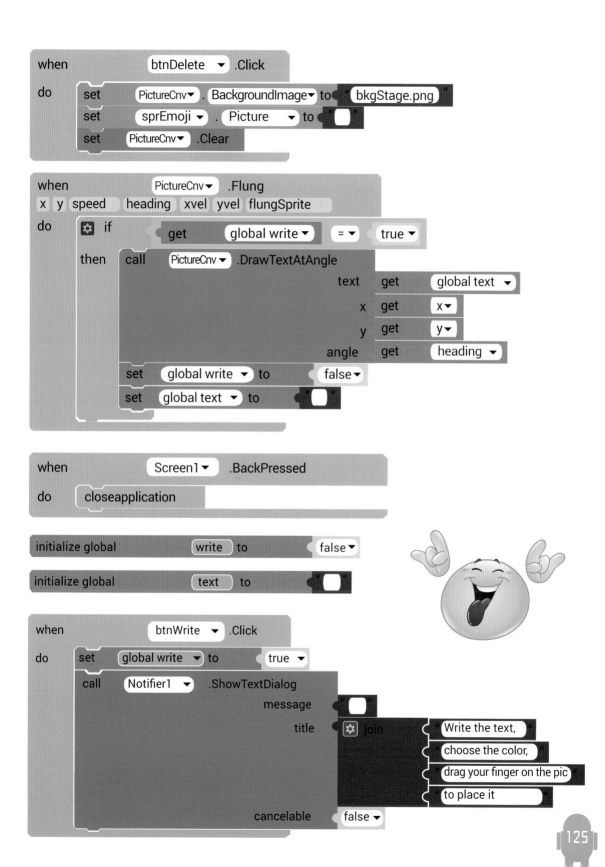

when btnDelete ▾ .Click
do set PictureCnv ▾ . BackgroundImage ▾ to " bkgStage.png "
set sprEmoji ▾ . Picture ▾ to " "
set PictureCnv ▾ .Clear

when PictureCnv ▾ .Flung
x y speed heading xvel yvel flungSprite
do ⚙ if get global write ▾ = ▾ true ▾
then call PictureCnv ▾ .DrawTextAtAngle
text get global text ▾
x get x ▾
y get y ▾
angle get heading ▾
set global write ▾ to false ▾
set global text ▾ to " "

when Screen1 ▾ .BackPressed
do closeapplication

initialize global write to false ▾
initialize global text to " "

when btnWrite ▾ .Click
do set global write ▾ to true ▾
call Notifier1 ▾ .ShowTextDialog
message
title ⚙ join " Write the text, "
" choose the color, "
" drag your finger on the pic "
" to place it "
cancelable false ▾

125

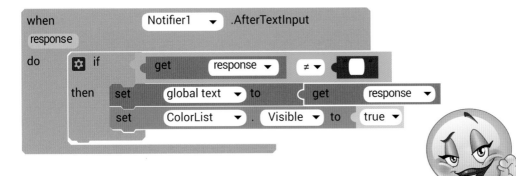

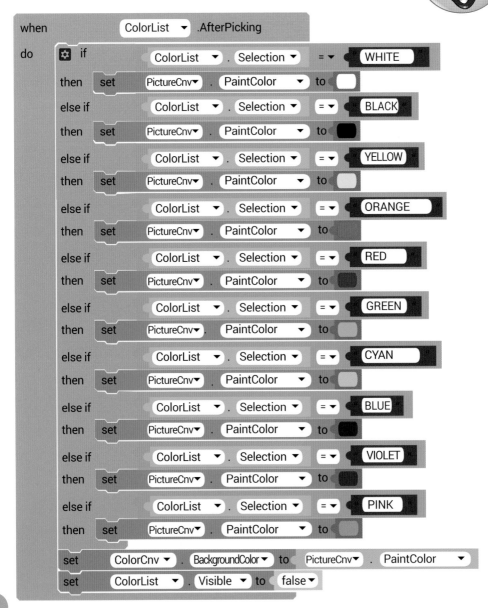

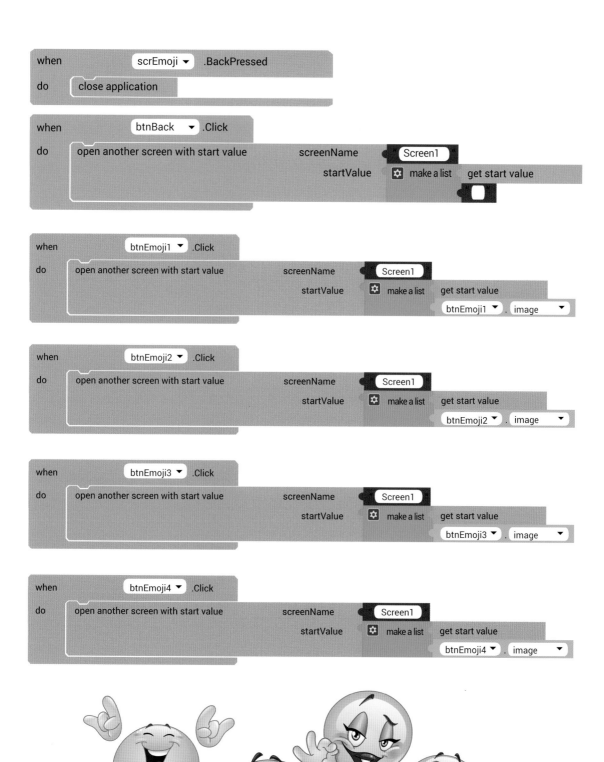

Monica Oriani Cauduro

After studying graphic design and earning a degree
in architecture, Monica has been a full-time
programmer for about twenty years.
Later she found out about CoderDojo and block
programming, Logo and robotics for kids.
Today she coordinates coding projects in schools
and summer camps for children aged 5 to 14.

White Star Kids® is a registered trademark property of
White Star s.r.l.

© 2019 White Star s.r.l.
Piazzale Luigi Cadorna, 6
20123 Milan, Italy
www.whitestar.it

Translation: Langue&Parole, Milan (Sara West)

ISBN 978-88-544-1529-4
1 2 3 4 5 6   23 22 21 20 19

Printed in Italy by Rotolito S.p.A.
Seggiano di Pioltello (Milan, Italy)